T0393157

Cambridge Elements ≡

Elements in the Global Middle Ages
edited by
Geraldine Heng
University of Texas at Austin
Susan J. Noakes
University of Minnesota–Twin Cities
Lynn Ramey
Vanderbilt University

TEACHING EARLY GLOBAL LITERATURES AND CULTURES

Geraldine Heng
University of Texas at Austin

CAMBRIDGE
UNIVERSITY PRESS

CAMBRIDGE
UNIVERSITY PRESS

Shaftesbury Road, Cambridge CB2 8EA, United Kingdom

One Liberty Plaza, 20th Floor, New York, NY 10006, USA

477 Williamstown Road, Port Melbourne, VIC 3207, Australia

314–321, 3rd Floor, Plot 3, Splendor Forum, Jasola District Centre, New Delhi – 110025, India

103 Penang Road, #05–06/07, Visioncrest Commercial, Singapore 238467

Cambridge University Press is part of Cambridge University Press & Assessment, a department of the University of Cambridge.

We share the University's mission to contribute to society through the pursuit of education, learning and research at the highest international levels of excellence.

www.cambridge.org
Information on this title: www.cambridge.org/9781009633048

DOI: 10.1017/9781009633062

© Geraldine Heng 2025

This publication is in copyright. Subject to statutory exception and to the provisions of relevant collective licensing agreements, no reproduction of any part may take place without the written permission of Cambridge University Press & Assessment.

When citing this work, please include a reference to the DOI 10.1017/9781009633062

First published 2025

A catalogue record for this publication is available from the British Library

ISBN 978-1-009-63304-8 Hardback
ISBN 978-1-009-63303-1 Paperback
ISSN 2632-3427 (online)
ISSN 2632-3419 (print)

Cambridge University Press & Assessment has no responsibility for the persistence or accuracy of URLs for external or third-party internet websites referred to in this publication and does not guarantee that any content on such websites is, or will remain, accurate or appropriate.

For EU product safety concerns, contact us at Calle de José Abascal, 56, 1°, 28003 Madrid, Spain, or email eugpsr@cambridge.org.

Teaching Early Global Literatures and Cultures

Elements in the Global Middle Ages

DOI: 10.1017/9781009633062
First published online: May 2025

Geraldine Heng
University of Texas at Austin

Author for correspondence: Geraldine Heng, heng@austin.utexas.edu

Abstract: *Teaching Early Global Literatures and Cultures* is a guide to the terra incognita of the global literature classroom. It begins with a framing rationale for why it is valuable to teach early global literatures today; critically surveys the issues involved in such teaching; supplies details of some two dozen texts from which to build a possible syllabus; adds a comprehensive bibliography, and suggestions for student research and student involvement in co-creating course content; and furnishes detailed guidelines for how to teach some ten texts. It should be possible for faculty and graduate instructors to take this Element and begin teaching its sample syllabus right away.

Keywords: global literature, race, Global Middle Ages, Orientalism, travel literature, world literature

© Geraldine Heng 2025

ISBNs: 9781009633048 (HB), 9781009633031 (PB), 9781009633062 (OC)
ISSNs: 2632-3427 (online), 2632-3419 (print)

Contents

1 Introduction: An Experiment in Learning – and Teaching – Early Global Literatures and Cultures

Anyone who has contemplated teaching a course on the literatures and cultures of the early global world has surely known a mix of emotions.

At first blush comes excitement and curiosity, perhaps a sense of mission. Teaching of this kind, after all, is still in its experimental stages, its infancy, and it is exciting to join a community committed to trying something intellectually new. But it must be said, this kind of teaching is also fraught with risk and the possibility of error. We are forced to confront the limitations of our training, our life experiences, our knowledge, and, frankly, our nerve. Part and parcel of the mix of responses is surely a degree of intimidation and anxiety, perhaps even a little fear.

But if you are reading this, you are likely someone drawn to the idea of continual self-learning, which teaching of this kind will ensure. Very probably, you see learning and teaching as mutually sustaining, conjoined processes, with that twinning being highly desirable. Already the first reward has arrived: You will acquire life-long learning far beyond anything your disciplinary training prepared you for, and you will never be bored. The teaching process, in the first instance, is then a learning process, as you and your students traverse the terra incognita of the global literature classroom together.

So, you accept, from the start, that no single person can be a thorough expert in the field of early global literatures and cultures – a specialist in all the literary and cultural texts and contexts that would be desirable to encounter, with students, in a classroom, whether of a brick-and-mortar kind or a virtual kind.[1] With that humbling recognition comes possibility: You will attempt to learn as much as you can, whenever you can, for the rest of your pedagogical life.

---

[1] Excitement and anxiety were the foremost emotions among the five faculty members (joined by two visiting faculty) at the University of Texas in Austin in spring 2004, when I devised an experimental six-to-nine-credit hour graduate course (attended also by two Plan II Honors undergraduates) to introduce the "Global Middle Ages," entitled "Global Interconnections: Imagining the World, 500–1500 CE." The term and concept of a "Global Middle Ages" grew out of preparing for, and reporting on, this course in 2003–2004. Interestingly, by 2012–2013, no anxiety was expressed by any faculty when I devised the year-long Winton Seminar at the University of Minnesota – Twin Cities, taught by seventeen visiting and on-campus faculty, "Early Globalities I: Eurasia and the Asia Pacific" (fall 2012) and "Early Globalities II: Africa, the Mediterranean, and the Atlantic" (spring 2013). Some thoughts and arguments in this Element adapt, revise, or reissue some of my earlier work, especially from *The Global Middle Ages: An Introduction* (henceforth, *GMA*), which inaugurates the multititle Cambridge Elements in the Global Middle Ages series, and two chapters of my MLA volume, *Teaching the Global Middle Ages* (henceforth, *Teaching*): "Introduction: What is the Global Middle Ages, and Why and How Do We Teach It?" and "The Literatures of the Global Middle Ages."

In researching an early global world, I've said in lectures and publications, *collaboration is key*: because you are not going to master within a single lifetime the spectrum of languages, knowledges, and disciplinary expertise you will need for global research.[2] In teaching, however, unless you are extraordinarily fortunate to be at an institution that welcomes and facilitates multi-instructor, collaborative teaching, you'll likely find yourself facing a classroom of students alone.

If we let the impossibility of full knowledge of our subject daunt us, we should stop here. When anxiety and intimidation remain the dominant emotions, we are likely never to accomplish a course on early global literatures.[3] For one, unlike world literature courses, there isn't a plethora of road maps and guides for solo-teaching of the literatures and cultures of the early global world. And there are certainly no Norton anthologies to serve as ballast for our syllabi.

This, in part, is because *global* literature is not the same thing as *world* literature (for which there are several Norton editions), though there are, of course, some convergences among texts. World literature courses tend to collect a miscellany of texts to represent the many cultures and localities of the world: to offer a snapshot of the world's literary creations in the form of best practices. Disparate texts can be plucked from many countries, many eras – sometimes across millennia – each of which serves to represent a place, a people, or a culture; an era, a style, a genre; or a particular type of author or society. The instructor must then find a way to stitch together some kind of course coherence – perhaps through themes, motifs, tropes, styles, genres, periods, and so forth – so as to assemble connections among a smorgasbord of texts that could range from the *Epic of Gilgamesh* to Lady Murasaki's *Tale of Genji* to Chairil Anwar's poetry to Chinua Achebe's novels.[4]

---

[2] Many Elements in our Cambridge series are authored by pairs or groups of specialists, sharing knowledges, resources, and skills. The Element on global textiles, *Medieval Textiles Across Eurasia c. 300–1400*, e.g., is authored by a Middle Easternist, a Sinologist-Eurasianist, and a Byzantinist, who pool their expertise on silk. *Teaching* also features pairs and clusters of specialists from different fields cowriting together.

[3] Or we can face our anxieties and power through, like the Islamicist in 2004, who nearly backed out at the last minute because of cold feet, but overcame her trepidation and became an enthusiastic advocate of early global studies. For a description of that 2004 seminar, and the coining of the problematic term and concept of a "Global Middle Ages," see my 2004, 2007, and 2009 essays, "Global Interconnections," "An Experiment," and "The Global Middle Ages."

[4] David Damrosch, editor of *Teaching World Literature*, puts it like this: "we seek to uncover a variety of compelling works from distinctive traditions, through creative combinations and juxtapositions guided by whatever specific themes and issues we wish to raise in a particular course" (9). Damrosch cautions, reasonably, "it's impossible to give equal time to every language, country, or century . . . world literature courses need to be exploratory rather than exhaustive" (9). Needless to say, global literature courses cannot be exhaustive either, but can be organized to explore key questions about globalism and the early global world, as the next sections suggest.

By contrast, global literature already arrives with a theme and connectedness: It thematizes the interconnectivities, the globalism, of early worlds. Whether the texts describe actual human travel, or show how a global religion arrives and reshapes local and regional lives, or demonstrate how art and artistry are exchanged along vast networks of trade, the texts of early globalism narrate interconnected worlds. They narrate with precision the intricate interconnectivity of the early world, and are produced by a multifarious world and its peoples. The texts are *windows* that open onto those interwoven, interknitted worlds.

This suggests another feature of global texts: Often, they do not offer themselves up as fiction or literary creations, but as accounts of how ordinary and extraordinary people lived their lives in the deep past, made their way in their world, and came to understand the environments and the societies they encountered.

Or they are reports of what people most valued – deeply held beliefs and ideas, remarkable art or important social practices, sought-after objects and goods – and how these came to interlink an early world. For that reason alone, students are often deeply curious about these texts, because they offer stories that not only open onto worlds, but stories that are lived worlds.

Sometimes, such texts even demonstrate global interconnectedness through their very composition: They demonstrate globalism by the way they have been assembled as a result of global transmission and accretion. One example is the co-created tale of Balaam and Josaphat, the story of the Buddha's life that, in the course of westward journeying from India over a millennium and a half, gradually metamorphoses – thanks to being handled and reshaped by various societies through which the story passes – into the tale of two Christian saints, by the time the story reaches the West. A much more famous exemplar, of course, is *The Thousand and One Nights*, *Alf Layla wa-Layla* (also known as *The Arabian Nights*), a migratory, accumulating body of stories that have been co-created for a millennium and more, well into modern time.

Still, unlike survey courses on world literature, there are no Norton anthologies of global literature on which to rely for teaching. Nor, perhaps, should there be: There is little reason why we cannot offer students many global texts in their entirety, with some exceptions of gloriously long texts that cannot be responsibly studied in their entirety within a span of weeks. In the sections that follow, I'll suggest texts that can be plumbed in entirety during a semester, and texts from which selections can responsibly be extracted.

Responsibly, here, is the key word. In teaching global literatures, a subject where we must surrender the pretense of mastery, we still have a duty – a *responsibility* – to learn as much as we can about the backgrounds, the historical and cultural contexts, styles, authors and authorial communities, that produced the texts we read in the classroom. We cannot throw up our hands that it's all too much: that it's impossible to learn enough to teach *Sundiata*, or the *Malay Annals*, or the *Secret History of the Mongols* with any degree of adequacy.

It is our responsibility to step outside our comfort zones, and incrementally, determinedly, extend our horizons of knowledge and learning as best we can. To aid us in this process is the reward of gradual familiarization: If you return to teaching early global literatures again and again, you will accrue incremental familiarity with the backgrounds and cultural contexts of your texts over time, and you can correct any possible earlier misapprehensions.

In this, your students can be allies. Students love nothing better than undertaking research. In lieu of requiring exams, quizzes, and tests, where students regurgitate what they have read, or what you have told them, consider asking for individual research presentations, and offering the possibility of collaborative projects where students conduct and share research and writing, an option I explore in Section 9 and elsewhere in this Element.

Students learn best when they are actively involved in hands-on work spurred by their own curiosity, interest, and preference – work of their own design – and, in the process, perform ownership of and shared responsibility for course content, which enables them to know that their contributions are valued as a significant and integral part of the course.

Whether your purview is literature, history, art history, or something else, there are also free aids in the form of online digital resources, such as Berkeley's ORIAS websites, the Global Middle Ages Project (G-MAP) platform, an increasing number of titles in the born-digital Cambridge Elements series (with each title downloadable for free, and sharable, the first two weeks after publication), as well as hard-copy guides like the MLA's *Teaching the Global Middle Ages*, or, if you prefer, old and new giant tomes of world-history surveys for broad-brush, rapid background sweeps of information.[5]

A caveat, however, as we consider the nonexistence of premade anthologies of literature and the imperative to step outside our comfort zones: In discussing the literatures of early globalism, I do not mean to suggest we should study what the world looks like through the eyes of Europe, as depicted in European literatures.

---

[5] For the ever-expanding list of Cambridge Elements, see www.cambridge.org/core/what-we-publish/elements/global-middle-ages. The G-MAP platform currently has nineteen digital projects and lists numerous online projects not associated with G-MAP (http://globalmiddleages.org/content/external). *Teaching* has comprehensive lists of online resources, in bibliographies, and the resources section. For ORIAS, see: https://orias.berkeley.edu/resources-teachers-0.

Yes, Chaucer's *Squire's Tale* mentions the name of Genghis Khan, and *Mandeville's Travels* purports to be about the real world "out there" when it issues its simulacra. Yes, the *Man of Law's Tale* has a fictitious woman fictively travel all over the Mediterranean, and the *King of Tars* fantasizes a Black sultan who turns white upon baptism.[6]

But teaching early globalism does not mean reissuing familiar texts that describe nonwestern worlds and peoples as these are fictionalized or imagined by Europe's authorial gaze. Reissuing European literature by the back door in this way, and rebranding Europe's canonical and familiar texts as *global literature* is merely eurocentrism by another name.

This is not to say, of course, that we shouldn't teach *a critical canon* of European literature, even as we teach *a counter-canon* of early global literatures. But we should not imagine that teaching European texts in a critical way is the same thing as teaching the global.

There are exceptional European texts, of course, that grant extraordinary views into far-flung worlds of their time, like Marco Polo's and Rustichello of Pisa's *Le Devisement du Monde* (The Description of the World) and early Franciscan reports of Mongol Eurasia and Yuan China, but these are exceptional historical accounts that decenter, rather than recenter the West, by virtue of the information they contain (whether or not the texts intend any decentering), and they can be useful additives in a global literature course. But we should remember that the purpose of teaching early global literatures is not to find new pretexts for reteaching Europe's universally, extensively taught texts under rebranded course rubrics.

2 Why Teach Early Global Literatures and Cultures?

What *is* the purpose of teaching global literatures then? For those of us concerned with the dominance of eurocentrism in university curricula, an important reason to teach global literature is that, by its very nature, it loosens and uncenters the grip of the West, provincializing Europe *avant la lettre* by being produced elsewhere, drawing attention to the multifarious lives and places in the world's many vectors.

In our current historical moment in the West, when white supremacists and ultra-nationalist extremists are busily fantasizing a glorified past in which so-called Christian-European values and civilization supposedly reigned triumphally in an idealized world of Christian domination, attention to the rest of the

---

[6] These examples are taught in English departments, but the reader can readily substitute European canons of their own. While Euromedievalists understand there wasn't a *Europe* in premodernity as such, and prefer *the Latin West*, *Christendom*, or other nomenclature, *Europe* remains a common heuristic in academic discussion, and is used as a placeholder of convenience here.

premodern world can be profoundly important.[7] Teaching the global can be a way to oppose pernicious ideological narratives of white-Christian-European supremacy and hegemony that purport to represent the deep past's historical truths, authenticity, and facticity.

When students learn that the city of London had 100,000 people and Paris had 200,000, at a time when Cairo had three-quarters of a million inhabitants, and a number of China's immense metropoles had populations of well over a million lives, an important shift in students' understanding of the past occurs, so that ethical, responsible recoveries of knowledge can begin.

The teaching of global literatures and cultures is then a process of *counter-narration* – an ethical imperative that opposes fantasies of a past where Europe took center stage in white societies of unfractured Christian homogeneity, while the histories and cultures of the rest of the world are forgotten and erased, rendered unimportant.

That such erasure and forgetting has pernicious effects is seen from a report by an African American medievalist, Cord Whitaker, who has been repeatedly asked, "Where *were* the Black people in the Middle Ages?" Apparently, Whitaker's "well-educated" interlocutors only knew of Africa from histories of slavery and colonialism in the modern era, and nothing of Africa's histories and cultures before the encroachments of the West. Given the outrageousness of such lacunae, teaching the stories and cultures of the early world – especially, in this case, Africa – can be an act of epistemological and ethical commitment.

Teaching of this kind can even correct the narratives of the well-intentioned left, along with the ideological fabulations of the extremist right. For instance, it is impossible to read premodern global literature without recognizing that for its texts, every place is the center of the world.

No person or polity in the epic of *Sundiata* considers the Empire of Mali to be positioned on the periphery of a great world-system whose economic and political center is hived elsewhere, not in Mali. The magnificent city of Vijayanagar, capital of the Indian empire of the same name in Kamaluddin Abdul-Razzaq Samarqandi's *Mission to Calicut and Vijayanagar*, is also the center of the world. Marco Polo's and Rustichello da Pisa's Hangzhou, surpassing other thirteenth-century megalopolises by its immensity of population, wealth, and cosmopolitanism, cannot be anything but the center of the world.

But it isn't just size, wealth, or fame that decides what gets to be the center of the world. For each text, the world turns on the axis of wherever its people and their lives are. Everywhere is the world's center. Global literature thus undercuts

---

[7] For a selection of essays on white supremacist fantasies of a glorified European past, see Kim, Lomuto, Rambaran-Olm and Rambaran-Olm and Wade.

well-intentioned economic models like world-systems analysis that systematize the world into centers and peripheries through economic or other rationales, and undoes assumptions of cultural superiority or priority that might be extrapolated from such organizational schemas.[8] Wherever the people are is the center of the world.

In the twenty-first-century classroom, where demographic and population changes in the West have created cohorts of students in higher learning who are substantially diverse in terms of their race, class, and countries of origin, the recognition that every place is the world's center acknowledges a multicentered – and thus, uncentered – world in which Europe assumes no special importance.

As significantly, for students whose ancestry, family origins, or childhoods were rooted in Africa, the Middle East, Asia, Latin America, Pacifica, and elsewhere, the global literature classroom is a way to encounter their countries of origin outside the West before the advent of European colonialism and imperialism in the modern eras. Students learn that history does not begin when Europe arrives.

Indeed, the sheer diversity of global texts, lives, cultures, cities, treasures, arts, technologies, trade, and networks in a thriving premodern world in which a Christendom-that-will-become-Europe is little more than a backwater by comparison, shifts the scales of comparison and understanding for students.

Learning that ninth-century Tang China had ceramic industries that were already mass-producing ceramic wares for export to the rest of the world by the tens of thousands, carried by ocean-going vessels that enabled the international demand for Chinese ceramics to be met, a millennium before the West's own mass-produced ceramics, thoroughly reconfigures a student's understanding of commercial revolutions that are defined only in western terms (see Heng, "An Ordinary Ship").

When a student learns that the tonnage of coal burnt in eleventh-century Song China's iron and steel industries was already roughly seventy percent of the tonnage of coal burnt in Britain's iron and steel industries at the beginning of the eighteenth century, the revelation that there could, in fact, have been *a number of industrial revolutions*, rather than a single, unique Industrial Revolution occurring only in modernity, and only in the West, is a mind-altering moment (see Hartwell, "Cycle," and "Revolution").

---

[8] I discuss world-systems analysis (originally devised by Immanuel Wallerstein as a critique of nation-and-state-based capitalism), including its core-periphery-semiperiphery economic model, in *GMA* 40–53, arguing that premodernists are not well served by extending world-systems analyses (with however good intentions) to premodernity.

For graduate students, one important outcome of learning globally is the incubation of new habits in thinking and research. Global learning fosters habits of reaching across cultures in the kinds of questions asked and the kinds of projects pursued. Even as departments and programs continue to ensure deep disciplinary training and knowledges, the aggregative process of global-local-regional training over time produces the happy result of distinctively new skills and professional identities for graduate students in what seems a perennially challenging academic market.[9]

Focusing on the global, of course, also works to bring medieval studies itself – a field that is still occasionally misunderstood by the rest of the academy as concerned largely with obscure interests mainly fascinating to academic antiquarians performing custodial functions for archives of little importance or urgency to anyone else – more visibly into conversation with other kinds of teaching, including contemporary globalization studies, in the twenty-first century academy.

Two decades ago, an article in the *Chronicle of Higher Education* showed what was at stake, by pointing to the dangers that lay ahead for a field whose interests were thought to be unimportant to the rest of the academy or society at large. In 2003, a journalist, Kate Galbraith, reported *The Guardian* quoting Charles Clarke, Great Britain's Secretary of State for Education at the time, facetiously intoning, "I don't mind there being some medievalists around *for ornamental purposes*, but there is no reason for the state to pay them" (emphasis added).

While medievalists in Britain were stung by this ignorant cabinet official's condescension, they also seemed to have difficulty arguing for their work's importance. Galbraith quoted a Cambridge medievalist falling back on an old vagueness, when she defended medievalists as "working on clarity and the pursuit of truth." The Cambridge scholar's lament that Clarke was "someone who doesn't understand what we do" touched on precisely the problem.

Nearly two decades later, the situation worsened: In 2021, the University of Leicester was reported as replacing its medieval literary curriculum with a decolonial curriculum prioritized by university administrators as urgently necessary in twenty-first-century England, thereby rendering the medievalists in Leicester's English department redundant (Johnston). Leicester's demand of a decolonial curriculum, we might note, could have been met with critical teaching of an early global world: a critical pedagogy that meets the objectives

---

[9] When I began writing this in fall 2022, NYU's English department advertised a tenure-track, entry-level position for a medievalist in early global literatures. Increasingly, entry-level recruitment of premodernists seems to stress as desiderata some degree of specialization in early global studies and/or early race studies.

of diversity, equity, and inclusion that have become important priorities in today's academy in the West.[10] Since 2021, other universities have also ended medieval programs (see, e.g., Cassidy).

3 Organizing a Course, and a Scaffold of Questions in Search of Answers

It is important to acknowledge, from the outset, that global literature can only be taught through textual translations. When David Damrosch leads a world literature class on *Gilgamesh*, we must assume that nobody is first required to learn Sumerian or Akkadian. The sample list of possible teaching texts I outline in Section 4 includes accounts in Old Norse, Mande/Mandingo, Arabic, Jawi/Malay, Chinese, Uighur-Mongolian, Latin, Syriac, Franco-Italian, and Hebrew: Any concatenation of global texts is going to be unteachable except through translations.

Thanks to the proliferation of translation theory in the academy, we are familiar, of course, with the problematics and politics of translation. We understand that every translation is a rewriting and a re-creation, not a facsimile or clone of the original that becomes replicated, with perfect exactitude, in another language. We recognize that translators make choices that can alter the sense of a word, a sentence, a passage; and that affect, meaning, and emphasis can all shift across the translational process.

Perhaps because we work with multiple languages, premodernists are among those who are most alive to the fact that any translation is never co-identical with the original from which it is reconstituted – if, that is, an original can even be determined, which is no sure thing in premodern literature. Inevitably, there will also be terms and concepts in all languages that we will deem utterly untranslatable.[11]

---

[10] Right-wing politicians in the West, in lockstep with white nationalists, have concomitantly introduced legislature to combat the ethical imperatives of diversity, equality, and inclusion in education, making critical teaching of the global even more urgent than before. On Leicester's neoliberal co-optation of the language of the left in announcing its decolonial curricular project, see Chaganti.

[11] We should also note power differentials among languages. Colonial and neocolonial languages like English, French, Spanish, *inter alia*, have been historically dominant because of imperialism, accruing cultural capital and prestige over the indigenous languages of dominated, colonized peoples. The languages of the Global North are considerably privileged over those of the Global South, but Casanova observes that nonwestern languages like Arabic, Chinese, and Hindi are also dominant because of their use by large populations (290). For "minority languages to survive ... they must have a presence, mostly through translation" (Baker 247, citing Cronin). Premodern languages resemble minority languages in some ways, since premodern forms of languages still in use – Chinese, Malay, etc. – are often unreadable by the untrained. Translation thus performs a service by ensuring accessibility to minority languages and older linguistic forms of nonwestern languages.

But the success of many translations-as-re-creations – from the King James Bible to Seamus Heaney's *Beowulf*, to name just two famous examples in the West – argues for the value of translations that evince cultural sensitivity, nuance, tact, and insight, as well as literary richness and genius.[12] More recently, Zrinka Stahuljak has argued for assessing a translation for its qualities of *commensuration*, not for its attempt at equivalence, so that equality, not exactitude, is the hallmark of translational success and effectiveness.[13]

Rather than seeing translation as a process of loss and distortion, we might then instead join the ranks of those who see translation as a creative, enlivening process that mediates between an original text and the new audiences to which the text would speak, and for whom it must become intelligible in order for its life and significance to continue. This is especially important for texts originally created in languages and dialects hundreds of years old, that can be accessed by fewer and fewer people today in their original languages.

We might join those who wish for *more* translations, so that the supply of available translations, and translational variety, can be enlarged, and a greater number, not a fewer number, of choices becomes available[14] – especially for instructors who might wish to conduct comparative linguistic study across translations and texts.[15] We may even hope that introducing students to texts they have never encountered before, through translation, might be a way to fascinate and to interest students in acquiring new languages.

So, rather than thinking of translation as something that must always detract from a text – and teaching in translation as disseminating imperfect, inexact replicas from which something is always missing or askew – we might see translation instead as the invitational dynamic that allows a text to acquire its fullest possible audience over time, as well as its widest possible range of significance for those audiences, as Damrosch urges (*How to Read* 5).

Without translations, premodern texts with few exceptions are easily neglected or forgotten, confined to their initial audiences who are distant in time and place.

---

[12] "Over eighty translations of *Beowulf* have appeared since the nineteenth century, but none has caught the reading public's attention as much as Heaney's" (Donoghue ix).

[13] See Stahuljak's remarkable presentation in "Multilingualism, Translation, Directionality in Global Medieval Digital Humanities," organized by Lynn Ramey and Dorothy Kim: http://globalmiddleages.org/content/panel-discussion-multilingualism-translation-directionality-global-medieval-dh.

[14] I owe this thought to a 2019 conversation with Huda Fakhreddine, who extolled the virtues of translation, and expressed a desire for more translations of Arabic literature ("as many as possible").

[15] I owe this thought to Nahir Otaño Gracia, who teaches Old Irish to her graduate students by having them compare various translations, while themselves translating Old Irish into modern English.

Noncanonical premodern texts are, of course, the most vulnerable, readily ignored and forgotten – especially, let's face it, in contemporary literature departments saturated with a multitude of modern literatures and the alluring creations of popular culture and digital media. By contrast, circulating early literatures through translations conduces to ensuring their continual reception across time, well into the future, and grants premodern texts long, rich, afterlives.

In this way, translation can be seen as imparting "a new stage in a work's life as it moves from its first home out into the world" (Damrosch, *How to Read* 84). We might even say that teaching with translations performs an exchange between the past and the present that parallels the sociocultural and geospatial exchanges so often thematized in global texts. This is a positive outcome of the fact that there can be no courses on global literatures (or world literatures) without translations.[16]

The actual texts we select for teaching a course on early global literatures and cultures will depend, of course, not only on the translations available to us, but also on what we want from the course. When I first began teaching early global literatures, a student asked, "What do you want us to know?" Her simple question went right to the heart of things. What the driving questions are, for you, will decide the texts you choose for your syllabus, and determine how you shape your course. Each person's answers will differ, and the discussions below are shaped by my own imperatives.

The broadest driving questions that scaffold my teaching of global literatures are the obvious ones: (1) Why does knowledge of the early world matter today? (2) What interconnects that early world? We know what interconnects the *modern* and *contemporary* worlds, but the *globalization* of the twenty-first century is not the *globalism* of premodernity.[17] (3) What does that early interconnected world look and feel like? This is an invitation to consider not just people, but climate, environment, towns and cities, topography, oceans, flora and fauna, and even how time is experienced. These large questions – each of which allows for finer-grained, detailed sub-inquiries – decide what texts are best suited to teaching a course.

Why does knowledge of the early global world matter? To combat Eurocentrism, and pernicious white supremacist fantasies. To end the ignorance

---

[16] This is not to say – lest it isn't blazingly obvious – that graduate students should cease to learn the various premodern languages that form a cornerstone of their programmatic education, but merely to acknowledge the impossibility of mandating that faculty and students – especially undergraduate students – acquire a dozen premodern languages first as a prerequisite to teaching or enrolling in a global literature course.

[17] For a critical discussion of why the term "globalization" makes little sense for premodernity, see *GMA* 33–40.

and atomization of knowledge that represents whole continents as without a history till Europe arrives. To critically decolonize the curriculum. To expand the horizons, skills, and opportunities of a graduate education. To be responsive to increasingly diverse twenty-first-century classrooms of global citizens. To ensure that a cultural archive of noncanonical, readily ignored texts are taught, and find contemporary audiences and significant afterlives. To end any lingering assumptions that premodern studies today represent obscure, ivory-tower indulgence in a world and an academy of shrinking resources. And more: Ultimately, the goal is the transformation of teaching in the twenty-first-century academy itself.[18]

What interconnects the early world? People in motion, for a variety of reasons; goods in motion; religions that spread; art and artistry in dynamic exchange; political and military power amassing territory. What did that interconnected world look and feel like? Answering this, leads us to global cities and how people lived and worked in them; to climate change and monsoons that enabled passage across oceans; or how the experience of time might involve counting the intervals between obligatory prayers, or the length of time it takes to read verses of the Quran.

Together, the questions remind us that the interconnectedness of an early world is not the planetary globalization of today, a globalization that – at least in theory – touches every part of our planet. Early globalism is not tantamount to, and should not be equated with, a twenty-first-century globalization that knits together, however unevenly, the inhabitants of all pockets of the planet.

Rather, we can conceptualize early globalism as a *push* for ever-larger scales of relation. The drive to invade, conquer, and occupy globalizes, but language also globalizes. Religion globalizes. Cultural habits, styles, artistic motifs globalize. Popular stories that travel widely globalize. Some forms of globalism in an early world are thus not spatial, or geographic, but assume a linguistic, artistic, religious, or cultural character.

We see, in this way, that early globalism involves not just a concept of interconnected, interrelated spaces and geographies, but also a *dynamic*: forces pushing toward larger and larger scales of relation.

The reminder of differences between the present and the past is helpful in a number of ways. For instance: A teacher or student of global literature should not feel a requirement to find texts addressing *every* place on the planet, nor feel a corollary obligation to establish the interconnectivity of each corner of the earth with every other corner of the earth through literature. The study of early globality is not synonymous with the study of planetarity.

---

[18] After the 2004 experiment, I was asked at lecture after lecture I delivered on the subject: Why can't learning be more often like this? So, yet another answer to Question 3 is, well, people *want* learning to be more often like this. See also Cathy Davidson on the transformation of the academy.

Though Europeans in the form of Greenlanders and Icelanders crossed the Atlantic Ocean to reach the North American continent around 1000 CE, they did not cross the Pacific Ocean to reach Austronesia. Though China's imperial "treasure ships" helmed by the Muslim eunuch admiral Zheng He crossed the Indian Ocean to reach Africa in the fifteenth century, they did not arrive in Austronesia, the Americas, or Antarctica. Extraordinarily, DNA research in plant biology now seems to indicate that Oceanic peoples traversed half the watery world to reach the South American continent, but there are no suggestions yet that the inhabitants of Oceania arrived in Siberia or Greenland. As new discoveries are made, of course, we can adjust syllabi to suit, but a totalizing comprehensiveness that must aim to envelope everything, everywhere, is neither the point nor the spirit of a global literature course.

For the present, the examples I suggest in the next section as one possible spectrum of texts to consider for critically investigating the interconnectivity of the early world will show early globalism at work as a dynamic and a force, as well as globalism in the more conventionally understood sense of interconnected spatialities and geographies.

When a religion like Islam makes its way out of the Hijaz in Arabia to West Africa, up the Volga to the Eurasian steppe, and into South Asia and island Southeast Asia, we can follow the pathways of early globalism by examining the tracery of a global religion's travels and its impact on local and regional societies as conveyed in textual accounts. Literature also shows globalism at work when Indic culture scatters across maritime Southeast Asia, spreading names and mythologies, along with Buddhism and Hinduism, all of which is highly visible in texts.

Literary texts also show *Pax Mongolica* famously securing overland trade routes and moving artisans and goods around the vast Eurasian continent from termini to emporia, so that an English king, Edward I, can wear Chinese brocade as part of his inauguration robes, and an Indian monarch at Vijayanagar, Deva Raya II, can wear a tunic of Zaytuni silk from Quanzhou, and fan himself with a Chinese fan, as reported by a Muslim diplomat from the Timurid empire. Continual experimentation will disclose myriad forms of globalism that may not be apparent until you begin the journey with students into the terra incognita of the global literature classroom.

4 What Should We Teach? Two Dozen Texts from Which to Extract a Possible Syllabus

To open windows onto an interconnected early world, I have a cluster of favorite texts that cycle in and out of my syllabi over the years, subject to change and substitution. Many other texts can be productively taught, of course, and this is just one possible concatenation among innumerable from which to choose. The selection combines well-known and less familiar texts, with translations available in English, but instructors located in French, German, Italian, Spanish, Chinese, Japanese, and other literature departments should be able to substitute appropriate translations in their own vernaculars.

After trial and error, this is the cluster of texts from which I currently extract a working syllabus:[19]

- *The Vinland Sagas: The Norse Discovery of America* (Magnusson and Pálsson; and/or Jones, *Eirik the Red and Other Icelandic Sagas*; and/or Kunz, "The Vinland Sagas")[20]: taught in full, and paired with *The Ice Hearts* (Bruchac) and *Skraelings* (Qitsualik-Tinsley) – novellas which imagine how Native North Americans might have viewed the settler-colonists of Greenlanders and Icelanders – and online exploration of the "'Discoveries' of the Americas" project on the G-MAP platform at www .globalmiddleages.org.
- *Sundiata: An Epic of Old Mali* (Kouyaté-Niane-Pickett); and/or *Sunjata: A New Prose Version*, by Condé-Conrad; and/or *The Epic of Son-Jara: A West African Tradition*, by Sisòkò-Johnson): taught in full, and paired with online exploration of the empire of Mali in the Zamani Project (https://zamani project.org), the Timbouctou Manuscripts Project (http://www.tombouctouma nuscripts.uct.ac.za), the "Caravans of Gold, Fragments in Time" exhibit at Northwestern University's Block Museum (https://www.blockmuseum.north western.edu/exhibitions/2019/caravans-of-gold,-fragments-in-time-art,-cul ture,-and-exchange-across-medieval-saharan-africa.html and https://www.you tube.com/watch?v=G6C_WCz67Dw) that emphasize the north–south gold

---

[19] To be useful to the largest number of educators, the discussion here assumes undergraduate teaching, but for Euromedievalists teaching graduate seminars, footnotes and bibliography point to some texts in their original languages. Where possible, I offer more than a single translation, to allow for flexibility of choice. The listed texts carry bibliographies of primary and secondary readings, discuss source materials, and offer contextual, historical, editorial, and background information, so for the most part, I do not list secondary readings, but am happy to suggest these, if readers write to me.

For those wanting broad-brush surveys of the world, several world history surveys exist. Though I no longer use these – they are expensive and require frequent repurchasing, with new editions reissued every few years – *Worlds Together, Worlds Apart* seems the most conceptually non-naïve. Chapters 5 and 6 of my *Invention of Race* (henceforth, *Race*) also discuss in detail some of the texts listed in this section: the *Vinland Sagas*, John of Plano Carpini's *History of the Mongols*, William of Rubruck's *Journey*, Rabban Sauma's journey to the Latin West, Polo-Rustichello's *Description of the World*, and various Franciscan letters and reports from Mongol Yuan China.

[20] For the original Old Norse, see Sveinsson and Þórðarson for *Grœnlendinga saga*, and Jansson for *Eiríks saga rauða*.

caravan routes of the Sahel and Sahara, in which Mali is prominent, alongside selected readings from the exhibition catalog of the same name, edited by Kathleen Bickford Berzock. Students may also consult, as needed, the Berkeley ORIAS website on *Sundiata* (which seems aimed at high school teachers: https://orias.berkeley.edu/resources-teachers/monomyth-heros-jour ney-project/sundiata).[21]

- *Ibn Battuta in Black Africa* (Hamdun and King), selections from accounts of the famous Moroccan traveler's sojourns in West Africa (extensively recounted by Ibn Battuta) and East Africa (parsimoniously recounted by him): paired with selected readings from *African Dominion: A New History of Empire in Early and Medieval West Africa* (Gomez) and Al-Jahiz's *The Book of the Glory of the Black Race* (Preston/Cornell; and/or *The Boasts of the Blacks Over the Whites*, Khalidi).
- Ibn Fadlan's *Mission to the Volga* (Montgomery, James E.; and/or *Ibn Fadlan's Journey to Russia: A Tenth-Century Traveler from Baghdad to the Volga River*, Frye): taught in full, with clips from the film *The Thirteenth Warrior* (for visual depiction of Nordic hygiene and funerary customs). Facing-page text in Arabic, in Montgomery's edition and translation of Ibn Fadlan, appears in *Two Arabic Travel Books*, a volume that also contains Abu Zayd al-Sirafi's *Accounts of China and India*, translated by Tim Mackintosh-Smith.
- Ibn Jubayr's travels around the Mediterranean: taught as selections from *The Travels of Ibn Jubayr* (Broadhurst), and paired with selections from Usama ibn Munqidh's *Book of Contemplation* (Cobb), and clips from *Kingdom of Heaven* (for visual depictions of architectural hybridity in the portrayal of Jerusalem and crusader territories, the famed "pincer movements" of Seljuk/ Arab militaries in the field, and the politics of coexistence under crusader occupation), with selections focusing on crusades/counter-crusades/holy war, and social-religious-cultural accommodations in life on the ground, as modalities of globalism in Syria, Palestine, Sicily, and the eastern Mediterranean.

---

[21] Since *Sundiata*, the epic recounting the formation of the great Empire of Mali, descends through centuries of oral narration by *griots/jeliw*, is still being performed in oral recitations today, and has only been set down in writing and translated in the modern era, there are many versions of the narrative. The Longman African Writers series version, narrated by Djeli Mamoudou Kouyaté and set down by Niane into French, then translated into English by Pickett, is the best known, most commonly taught, and rich in detail, containing the most core episodes of the narrative tree, but is not a direct transcription from a single performance by a griot/jeli. The *Norton Anthology of World Literature*'s extract is from the Condé-Conrad translation (an abridged transcription from an oral performance, with several parts of the oral narration omitted). The Sisòkò-Johnson translation (*Epic*) stresses orality and performance much more than the other two translations, is ethnographically rich and informative, and has a comprehensive companion edition with a dual-page translation in Mande and English (*Son-Jara*), but will be more opaque to students, who will need greater guidance. For a compact teaching guide, see Gomez's chapter in *Teaching*; his *African Dominion* has three chapters on Mali, including one on Sunjata.

- *The Arabian Nights* (Haddawy; and/or *Tales from the Thousand and One Nights*, Dawood; and/or *The Arabian Nights*, Heller-Roazen and Haddawy; and/or *The Annotated Arabian Nights*, Seale): taught as a series of rotating selections that are chosen for different emphases in different iterations of the syllabus.[22]

- Buzurg ibn Shahriyar's *The Book of the Wonders of India: Mainland, Sea and Islands* (Freeman-Grenville): a lesser-known compendium of accounts and tales by mariners, attributed to a sea-captain of Ramhormuz, that can be taught in full, and is excellent for comparison with the fictional sea-oriented stories in *The Arabian Nights* such as *Jullanar of the Sea*, *The Third Dervish's Tale*, and *The Tale of the First Lady* in *The Story of the Porter and the Three Ladies*. Also useful for comparing with sea journeys in nonfictional texts – sea-travel stretches across several texts in this cluster – and with accounts of caravan journeys across the Eurasian landmass.

- Documents from the Cairo Genizah – in particular, a selection from *India Traders of the Middle Ages* (Goitein and Friedman) featuring the business transactions, agents, and relationships of the Jewish India trader Abraham ben Yizu – paired with Amitav Ghosh's *In an Antique Land: History in the Guise of a Traveler's Tale* and Ghosh's *Subaltern Studies* article, "The Slave of MS. H.6": These texts, which narrate the movement of goods and people between North Africa and India, include a focus on Ghosh's attempt to recover, from the anonymity of history, the name and identity of an enslaved South Asian man on the Malabar coast who functioned as ben Yizu's business agent in the twelfth-century Indian Ocean trade. The texts thus form an important corrective to narratives of empire-formation and imperial history that tend to feature prominently in archives of texts that survive (including the ones listed here) and constitute a key way to demonstrate to students how importantly histories-from-below, and microhistories, can contribute to our understanding of early globalism.

- Kamaluddin Abdul-Razzaq Samarqandi's *Mission to Calicut and Vijayanagar* (Thackston): taught in full, and containing a spectacular description of a premodern global city – Vijayanagar – with detailed portrayals of the city's infrastructure, layout, and architecture, its markets and vendors, elephantorium, mint, and bordello, complete with festivals and spectacles, and

---

[22] *The Arabian Nights*, and *Proclaiming Harmony* are the only two fictional texts in this basket of sample texts from which to build a syllabus. The *Nights* features historical figures like Harun al-Rashid and his bodyguard Jaffar, but highly fictionalized; the Syrian manuscript forming the basis of Haddawy's translation is usefully punctuated by references to culture and society during the three-centuries-long Egyptian-Syrian Mamluk dynasties. Like the *Nights*, *Proclaiming Harmony* was popular with audiences in its time, but under-appreciated by literati and intellectual elites.

the Muslim diplomat-narrator's account of India's port cities, the hazards of sea travel, flora and fauna, temple art and architecture, and featuring pungent ethnoracist commentary on South Asians.

- Selections from the *Sejarah Melayu* or *Malay Annals* (Brown): a chronicle-cum-epic depicting the cultural and mythological relations between India and island Southeast Asia, especially as transacted through the global Alexander legend, with storied accounts of the web of sea-borne interrelationships among the island-polities of maritime Southeast Asia. My selection begins at the beginning and ends at the point of the formation of the Malacca Sultanate, including the formation of the port-city of Temasek (premodern Singapore), and the dynamic movement of prestige and power among these island-societies and kingdoms in a world dominated by seas and water.[23]

- Abu Zayd al-Sirafi's *Accounts of China and India* (Mackintosh-Smith, with facing-page text in Arabic): taught in full, and paired with online exploration of the Tang Shipwreck exhibit at the Asian Civilisations Museum in Singapore (http://globalmiddleages.org/project/tang-shipwreck): This is a handbook of ninth- and tenth-century merchants' accounts, primarily of China, but also of India, compiled in two books, the first attributed to Sulayman al-Tajir (Sulayman the Merchant), and the second claimed as Abu Zayd's. Excellent for comparison with other merchants' accounts of China and India, like Polo-Rustichello's *Description of the World*; fictional stories of mercantilism and travel in *The Arabian Nights*; and other texts in this cluster like the *Malay Annals*, and *Mission to Calicut and Vijayanagar* for descriptions of islands and seas, coastal ports, and merchandise. Exploration of the Tang Shipwreck helps to bring alive the ships (including hand-sewn ships, without nails), cargoes, and peoples described by Abu Zayd.

- *Proclaiming Harmony* (Hennessey): recommended to me by the Sinologist Valerie Hansen, and taught in full, to introduce students to the repeating phenomenon of premodern China's history of invasions-and-displacements through a fourteenth-century semi-fictional dramatization of historical events that occurred two centuries earlier: featuring the disastrous reign of Huizong, the last emperor of the Northern Song dynasty and his profligate, debauched rule, his trust in corrupt, inept officials, and his eventual captivity and deportation, along with his son and their wives, to Manchuria, by the

---

[23] The *Malay Annals* is another text that was orally transmitted and written down late, with the oldest manuscript appearing in the modern era. See Derek Heng's chapter in *Teaching;* for historical background on networks in Southeast Asia, see his Cambridge Element, *Southeast Asian Interconnections.*

Juchen conquerors who formed the Jin dynasty before the advent of the
Mongols.

- *The Secret History of the Mongols: A Mongolian Epic Chronicle of the
  Thirteenth Century* (de Rachewiltz, 3 vols; and/or *The Secret History of the
  Mongols*, Atwood), paired with *Mongol: The Rise of Genghis Khan* (Bodrov):
  The first three chapters can be taught in undergraduate courses; graduate
  students can read the full text. The full text, in volume 1 of de Rachewiltz, is
  available online as an open-access book of 268 pages (de Rachewiltz's print
  version of vol. 1 is 642 pages long): https://cedar.wwu.edu/cgi/viewcontent
  .cgi?article=1003&context=cedarbooks. Volume 2 comprises invaluable historical, contextual, stylistic, and background apparatuses, and a supplementary
  volume 3 has an updated commentary, revisions, and some new interpretations.
  A Penguin translation, by Christopher Atwood, was published in late 2023.
  Mongol, the first of Sergei Bodrov's three-part film series, is useful to help
  students visualize the landscapes, environment, clothing, and customs of the
  Mongols, and for listening to the Mongolian language and throat-singing. The
  sequel, *Mongol II: The Legend*, is being financed for production at the time of
  my writing.[24]
- John of Plano Carpini's *History of the Mongols* (Dawson, *Mission to Asia* 1–72):
  taught in full, together with Dawson's introduction (vii–xli), "Two Bulls of Pope
  Innocent IV Addressed to the Emperor of the Tartars" (Dawson 73), "Guyuk
  Khan's Letter to Pope Innocent IV" (Dawson 85), and an extract from chapter 6
  of *Race* ("The Mongol Empire: Global Race as Absolute Power") on the
  Hystoria Mongalorum (287–302).
- William of Rubruck's *Journey* (Dawson, *Mission to Asia* 89–220; and/or
  Jackson and Morgan's *The Mission of Friar William of Rubruck: His Journey
  to the Court of the Great Khan Mongkë 1253–1255*): taught in full, together
  with the letters of Franciscan missionaries to China – John of Monte Corvino,
  Peregrine of Castello, and Andrew of Perugia (Dawson 224–237) – and an
  extract from chapter 6 of *Race* ("The Mongol Empire: Global Race as
  Absolute Power") on William of Rubruck (298–323).[25]

---

[24] Bodrov's *Mongol* was recommended to me by the late Thomas Allsen, a distinguished historian
of the Mongol empire, as a culturally rich, visual and auditory aid for teaching, despite the
ahistoricity of certain episodes and scenes (which will be clear to students as they read *The Secret
History*). If you would like his unpublished review of *Mongol*, please email me. I sometimes also
offer students the modern docudrama, *The Story of the Weeping Camel*, to help them understand
the intimate relationship the peoples of the steppe have with animals and the arts, especially
music.

[25] For the Latin texts of John, William, and the Franciscans in Dawson, see Wyngaert. Standaert's
Handbook of Christianity in China is useful to consult on the Franciscans in Yuan China and
clerics of the Church of the East ("Nestorians") such as Rabban Sauma. A hefty 964 pp. long, it is
considerably more recent than Moule and extends to the post-Mongol Ming and Qing dynasties.

- Rabban Sauma's journey to the Latin West (Borbone; also translated by James A. Montgomery; by Budge; and excerpted as chapter 4 of Moule), recounting the journey of a Uighur/Ongut monk/priest/envoy named Sauma, of the Church of the East (the so-called "Nestorian" Church) – whose one-time fellow-sojourner, Mark, aka Yaballaha or Jabalaha, became Patriarch of the Church of the East – as Sauma journeyed to the Latin West.[26] Sauma had polite discussions-that-seemingly-did-not-amount-to-disputations with the Curia in Rome, visited shrines and relics, was blessed and given gifts and honors by Pope Nicholas IV, and performed a mass of the Eastern rite in Gascony in 1288 attended by Edward I of England, who took communion at the hands of Sauma – a churchman who, under other conditions, would likely have been considered a heretic by the thirteenth-century Latin Church.[27]
- Marco Polo-Rustichello of Pisa's *Description of the World* (Moule and Pelliot; and/or Latham, *The Travels of Marco Polo*; and/or Kinoshita): taught in full and paired with the sections on Polo-Rustichello in chapter 6 of *Race* ("Marco Polo in a World of Differences"), 323–349. Though long, this European text coauthored by a Venetian merchant and an Italian romancer decenters the West to such an extent and is so detailed in its global description of goods, peoples, and lands that it is worth teaching in entirety. Also, merchant accounts form an important counterpoint to accounts by religious personnel and diplomats, and accounts about warriors and empire-formation that may otherwise dominate a syllabus.[28]

---

[26] The "Persian original ... is only known through an abridged Syriac translation" (Moule 94). Accounts in European languages are thus subject to double- or triple-translation. Borbone's 2021 edition and translation from the Syriac – the fullest, most recent, featuring facing-page Syriac and English – is translated from Italian into English by Parodi. Budge, and James A. Montgomery, are based on the Syriac, while Moule is based on a French translation from the Syriac. Hackett will publish Thomas Carlson's revision of Borbone, in a text intended for teaching, in September 2025. For a concise discussion of Sauma, see *Race*, 373–375 ("Journey to the West: Rabban Sauma, a Nestorian Heretic, in Latin Christendom").

[27] Those who teach global pilgrimage and want texts beyond the Abrahamic religions and Europe/ the Mediterranean/Islamic West Asia, might consider the accounts of East Asian Buddhist monks who make the long, hazardous journey to South Asia, seeking sacred learning from Buddhism's home, India. Faxian, and Xuanzang, from China, and Hyecho, from Korea, are excellent examples. For an English translation of Faxian, see Legge; for Xuanzang, see Li Rongxi; for Heycho, see Yang et al., and Whitfield-Wegehaupt.

[28] The popular Penguin translation by Latham intercalates materials from several manuscripts, containing episodes, characters, and events absent from Kinoshita's accessible translation of a single manuscript, the Franco-Italian. Penguin classics are inexpensive (used copies can cost less than a dollar), but Moule-Pelliot and Kinoshita are useful for graduate courses, since the former incorporates all the major manuscripts in its translation and supplies marginal glosses and notes, and the latter is helpful for teaching the Franco-Italian manuscript (for the original Franco-Italian, see Ronchi).

The preceding texts are most useful for my current purposes in devising a syllabus, but the following texts are also excellent to consider.[29]

- Benjamin of Tudela's *Itinerary* (Adler)[30]
- Selections from Ata-Malik Juvaini's *Genghis Khan: The History of the World Conqueror* (Boyle)
- Rashid al-Din's *The Successors of Genghis Khan* (Boyle)
- Selections from Ibn Battuta's *Travels* (Gibb)

5 What Interconnects the Early World? What Does that Early World Look Like? Teaching *The Vinland Sagas, Sundiata: An Epic of Old Mali*, and Ibn Fadlan's *Mission to the Volga* as Global Texts

Observant readers will notice that the texts listed in Section 4 more or less move students across the globe from west to east, starting with North America, and ending with China, after visiting trans-Saharan Africa, Eurasia, North Africa, the Mediterranean, South Asia, and Southeast Asia. This is partly an organizational idiosyncrasy – another instructor may prefer to have texts advance chronologically or thematically – and partly a preference born of students' satisfaction at seeing themselves literally proceed across the world with each reading.

This and the next sections go on to discuss ways to teach some ten texts combed from the basket of teachable texts in Section 4, augmenting the discussion with references to additional texts that, because of an Element's word limitations, cannot be treated in detail. For reasons of length limitations, I concentrate on issues of globalism, and the aims identified in the preceding sections as of particular urgency or significance, leaving aside more literary considerations to subject specialists of these texts cited in notes and the bibliography.[31]

---

[29] Though there's abundant European travel literature, very few European texts have been listed in this cluster, to avoid recentering Europe's authors – including popular texts of fiction/fantasy such as *Mandeville's Travels* (now a staple in so many syllabi).

[30] Adler's 1907 critical edition has the text in Hebrew, with an English translation, and indices in Hebrew and English. The 1983 imprint has additional introductions by A. Asher, and Michael A. Signer. Useful guides include Marci Freedman's and Eva Haverkamp-Rott's chapters in *Teaching*.

[31] The discussion assumes an undergraduate class. Graduate students are asked to read more critical and cultural theory, and, since they are being trained to *teach* global courses of this kind, they are also asked for book reports on extra texts that cannot be included in class, and additional focal considerations that pertain to them. Given that graduate students enroll from all programs and departments across campus, they are also asked to read the texts in their original languages, whenever possible.

To my regret, the texts listed in Section 4 focus primarily on narrative, written literatures (including accounts finally written down after centuries of orature), and so bracket for now the globalisms of Mesoamerica, Austronesia, Native America, and Oceania (nonetheless, island worlds are here represented by the *Malay Annals*). I've noted, of course, that teaching *the global* in premodernity need not be tantamount to teaching *the planetary*, but others might wish to consider materials studied by art historians, archeologists, and historical anthropologists, and treat inscriptions, epigraphs, law codes, folklore/legends/myth, among other cultural resources, as varieties of global literature.[32]

In classroom teaching, I begin by telling students we are guided by a set of focal points that become incrementally elaborated as the semester advances. I ask students to keep an eye on those focal issues that particularly interest them, as they read text after text, so that by the semester's end, they will have acquired a rich comparative perspective across the world's cultures.

The focal questions begin like this: What does globalism look like in a given text? How is the unknown represented in global encounter? How are otherness and difference represented? Do climates and ecoscapes elicit types of human responses that repeat across the world? How are women treated, what are their roles, and are there similarities across cultures? What constitutes wealth or treasure for a society? How is a society organized, and what are its values? What kinds of animals, plants, tools, arts, and occupations seem to matter the most? What particular colors, directions, rituals, and customs are given special significance? And, not least of all, what bridges exist across differences and incomprehension in global encounter?

I warn students there will be disorientation as we move across the world, repeatedly encountering new strings of names and naming traditions, strange environments, unfamiliar social and cultural mores, perplexing forms of magic or the supernatural, metaphysical or religious beliefs antithetical to their own, as well as literary and narrational styles and genres that will change with every text.[33]

Usually, literature majors and minors can reliably be counted on to use the close reading skills they've acquired to engage with the texts we read. If they feel overwhelmed by a mass of details, I ask them to follow the main characters, and the primary arc or arcs of narrative as a practical measure, and to raise

---

[32] I thank a reviewer of this Element for reminding me of the usefulness of including this paragraph.

[33] In the spring 2004 global course, where students and faculty met intensively for six hours a week, students never sat in the same seat twice around the seminar table. While they rapidly acclimated to being mentally shunted around the world, absorbing new bodies of knowledge weekly, the fact that none of them ever sat in the same seat twice perhaps suggested a vestigial disorientation that kept them physically moving, as they were being intellectually moved along in the course.

questions when something is so unclear that they have not been able to ferret out its meaning after trying.

I explain that I will not be able to answer every question they have, and they should expect to do research, and find answers of their own, to share with the class. But I also tell them they should never hesitate to ask questions for fear of looking foolish or ignorant – because, in the terra incognita of the global literature classroom, there are no bad questions. No questions are out of bounds.[34]

"What do you want us to know?" a student once asked on the first day of class, preempting the question I usually ask them, *what do you want from this class*?

I tell students I'd like them to know that globalism (to be distinguished from our contemporary *globalization*)[35] did not begin in the modern era, nor with European colonial maritime expansionism and "discovery" across the world. Cosmopolitan global cities like Vijayanagar, Cairo, and Quanzhou dwarfed the towns of Latin Christendom/Europe; supernovas were charted in eleventh-century China; the number zero had appeared in Indian mathematics by the seventh century; and linear algebra had been invented outside the West by the thirteenth (Hart).

Understanding that thriving, nonwestern cultures and civilizations existed, and were in dynamic interchange for centuries and millennia, undercuts *grands récits* about modernity and the West that have been cloned and recloned in the academy and public culture for generations, and gives the lie to alt-right fantasies of a dominant Christian Europe whose assumed supremacy relegates the rest of the early world to erasure.

So, to begin.

The Vinland Sagas: The Greenlanders' Saga and Eirik the Red's Saga

Beginning with the *Vinland Sagas* and Nordic journeying from eastern Greenland across the Atlantic to North America highlights an important focal question: *Why* did premodern peoples travel, given the extreme hazards and sometimes near-impossibilities of long-distance journeying? Student responses, partly conditioned by Hollywood and television, will include: a desire for exploration, a love of adventure and discovery, and "because it's there."

According to the *Sagas*, however, the motives of the would-be settler-colonists in "Vinland" – North American regions believed to be somewhere in

---

[34] Of course, students' freedom to ask anything, or to comment, does not license hate speech, bigotry, or attempts to shut down others.

[35] See *GMA*, 33–40.

New Brunswick, around the Gulf of Saint Lawrence and the Miramichi River, though excavation has thus far only unearthed the settlers' gateway or staging post at L'Anse aux Meadows in Newfoundland – involve *resource extraction*.[36] While a mix of reasons may have prompted the journeys – from characteristic patterns of Nordic settler-colonization, to individual and communal impulses – the *Sagas* usefully establish *the profit motive* as an impelling prompt.

The *Sagas* depict a North America around 1000 CE teeming with rich natural resources: timber from tall trees absent in Greenland and essential for boatbuilding and homesteads; wild grapes for making wine, a high-value prestige product usually requiring importation from the Mediterranean; "wild wheat" (a kind of rye?) growing unbidden, without the need for cultivation; fish fat in tidal pools when the tide went out; and a climate so mild in Vinland's southern outpost, even in winter, that livestock could conveniently be kept outdoors (56–57, 65, 95, 98).[37]

In addition to the land's Edenic natural resources, the *Sagas* also relate how the Indigenous peoples of North America proffer valuable furs and pelts in trade for what the settlers extend – sips of milk, or strips of red cloth (65, 99). Accordingly, the *Greenlanders' Saga* (henceforth, *GS*) shows Thorfinn Karlsefni, co-leader of the most prominent North American expedition, growing wealthy from his Vinland enterprise. Disembarking in Norway after departing Vinland, Karlsefni unloads and sells his furs, pelts, and other Vinland treasures – including a ship's figurehead carved from North American wood – for a small fortune, thereafter buying a farm and homestead in Iceland where his and his wife's descendants (which include three bishops) live for generations thereafter.[38]

The profit motive, students begin to see, is a theme that runs through global texts. While humans may indeed desire adventure and exploration, *profit* is a reliable instigator of trans-world journeying, despite all hazards and risks. The *Sagas* also introduce the idea that what is considered valuable, and constitutes wealth, assumes different forms in different places. Timber and grapes (and wine made from grapes) are not palpably forms of wealth in students' lives today, though these are animating attractions for the earliest visits to the North American continent. Students may find imagining a world where lumber is scarce a worthwhile thought experiment.

---

[36] For the archeological excavations at L'Anse, a national historic and UNESCO world heritage site and a full discussion of the *Sagas*, see *Race*, chapter 5.

[37] Page numbers refer to Magnusson and Palsson. *Race* (chapter 5) supplies additional bibliographic, critical, and other scholarly information.

[38] Glaumbaer, Thorfin Karlsefni's and Gudrid Thorbjarnardóttir's homestead, has been extensively excavated. Students may enjoy Nancy Marie Brown's biography of Gudrid as supplementary reading.

Beginning a global literature course with the *Vinland Sagas* also at once raises the paramount role of *climate* and atmospheric phenomena in shaping early globalism. In the eleventh century, a period of global warming dubbed the Little Climatic Optimum, the Medieval Climate Anomaly, or the Medieval Warm Period (among other names) increased the temperature in circumpolar regions by a few degrees, thereby enabling the Atlantic to be traversable in summer months.[39]

Students may notice on their own that even after the settler-colonists are routed by native Indigenous populations in pitched battles, and decide to abandon their settlements, the *Sagas* show they do not leave till summer arrives, but merely hunker down in their more northerly camp, where no Indigenous are ever encountered, till the weather allows for departure.

They should also be told that Greenland, from which the European settler-colonists sailed, would itself be abandoned during the Little Ice Age that arrived in the fourteenth and fifteenth centuries, leaving Greenland habitable only by the Inuit, whose lifestyles were adaptable to late-medieval climate change. Climate change is an issue close to students' minds, as their generation inherits the Anthropocene created by earlier generations and ours, and the *Sagas* bring home the impact of climate on human lives.

Indeed, students will encounter the impact of climate and atmospheric conditions again and again in the semester's readings. Journeying from the Abbasid Caliphate up the Volga, the Arab emissary Ibn Fadlan is taken aback by how his beard freezes in the cold after his bath, and how layers of clothing necessary for warmth obstruct his being able to move on his mount. But while atmospheric conditions pose challenges, they can also awe: The aurora borealis is a marvel Ibn Fadlan beholds, an extraordinary spectacle to be experienced in a lifetime.

In other texts, students will see how the weather phenomenon of winds known as the *monsoons* (from Arabic, *mawsim*, "season") decides in which direction a ship can sail across the Indian Ocean and South China Sea, and during which months of the year. Diplomats, merchants, and sailors are stranded in ports, awaiting the right winds to blow from the right direction, before they can complete their missions and enterprises. The impact of climate and weather upon human ambitions and human activity is a repeating, sometimes sobering lesson.[40]

---

[39] Climate change of this kind did not uniformly impact the world; e.g., climate scientists tell us that the rise in temperatures did not affect the Mediterranean region in the way it did the subpolar regions.

[40] Ibn Jubayr's despair at uncooperative weather in his tumultuous sea travels around the Mediterranean is especially heartfelt (Broadhurst 329–338, 361–363).

Crises and exigencies that arise are shown to elicit a range of human responses. In premodernity, many responses involve explanations issuing from religious faith, especially among people espousing the Abrahamic confessions. In the *Sagas*, clashes between Christian and "pagan" viewpoints furnish opportunities to discuss the spread of global religions like Christianity, and how the arrival of a global religion changes local behavior, but also meets with resistance.

Eirik the Red's Saga (henceforth, *ESR*) has an episode of hunger in Vinland where those who follow Thorhall the Hunter and eat the flesh of a "whale" that washes ashore at the northerly outpost of Straumfjord – a food source Thorhall glosses as a reward from the Norse god Thor – fall violently ill. Those who abstain from eating the animal and pray to Christ instead are rewarded with good weather and good fishing soon afterward (95–96). Christianity wins, here and elsewhere in the *Sagas*, as a new global religion is shown successfully to displace older faith traditions.

But *ESR* also describes a famine in Greenland, and how a sorceress, Thorbjorg, is invited to Herjolfsness to prophesy the future to anxious homesteaders. Treated with great deference, her outlandish appearance and demands meet with no hint of criticism, and even possibly a touch of awe. When the sorceress calls for old warlock songs to be sung, an opportunity is created to demonstrate possession of deep pagan knowledge by Gudrid Thorbjarnardóttir, Karlsefni's important wife-to-be, yet also Gudrid's strong commitment to Christianity, signaled by her initial refusal to perform the songs. Eventually, after singing the warlock songs beautifully, Gudrid is rewarded with sorcerous prophecy of an eminent lineage to issue from her (81–83).

Students quickly see Gudrid's consent to performing old pagan songs, despite her initial reluctance, as essential to her characterization as someone who is the ideal woman in her society – a good Christian reluctant to perform forbidden pagan knowledge, but whose commitment to hospitality and civility is overriding, and ultimately allows her to behave like a wise woman bestriding old and new worlds, possessing wisdom in both.

Gudrid's role in the *Sagas* thus offers an opportunity to begin a discussion thread on the roles of *women* in early global texts. Both *GS* and *ESR* highlight episodes where male settler-colonists, on encountering the Indigenous peoples of the Americas, gratuitously kill them, cheat them, and commit various kinds of violence. I discuss these episodes in detail in *Invention of Race* (chapter 5), and will refrain from rehearsing the discussion here, except to say that these episodes form prime examples of a racializing dynamic seen to occur in early global texts when members of one civilization encounter members of another civilization who seem wholly foreign to them.

Native North Americans are presented in the *Sagas* as primitive peoples fascinated with the superior metal technology of the expeditioners' weapons, and as naifs ignorant of the value of their furs and pelts in the international circuits of commerce to which the expeditioners have access. The racialization of Indigenous peoples thus turns not only on their physical appearance – facial features, hair, coloring, clothing – but also on the assumption that the Indigenous are located relatively low on a socio-evolutionary ladder of civiliza-tional maturity. (That the expeditioners are nonetheless routed by the natives in pitched battles is an embarrassment the *Sagas* do not address.)

Themes of comparative civilizational maturity are introduced again and again in texts of global encounter. The *Sagas* usefully lend themselves to addressing this thematic early in the semester.

Revealingly, an episode in *GS* featuring Gudrid serves up a counterexample to the masculine violence on display in the *Sagas*: Gudrid is sitting by the door of her home, peaceably rocking her new infant son Snorri in his cradle, when a Native woman appears in the doorway. Gudrid, who has been described as not only beautiful but also intelligent, and someone who knows well how to behave, asks the Native woman for her name; says her own name first; and, when the Indigenous woman echoes her words, hospitably gestures to her visitor to come and sit down beside her.[41]

The tranquil domestic scene ends abruptly, however, when a loud crash occurs outside (predictably, one of Karlsefni's men has killed a native), and the woman promptly vanishes.

Here, it's worth asking students: After generations of cultural transmission through which communal memories of the Vinland expeditions were narrated before they were set down in writing, who would have wanted an episode like this to exist, and why? What is accomplished, when a counterpoint to masculine bellicosity is created with a domestic setting in a woman's home, with a mother rocking her baby? We can have students consider how women are made to carry symbolic significance for a society, including today – whether the symbolism is of a mother with an infant, or a woman wearing hijab, or a woman sporting battle fatigues.

The *Sagas* do not, however, essentialize women as peacemakers and consist-ently unlike violent men. *GS* portrays a sanguinary, murderous woman, Freydis – Leif Erickson's (half?) sister – and *ESR* has a Valkyrie-like, pregnant Freydis terrify Native Americans by beating a naked sword against her bared breast. Often, students are quick to see that the portrayal of a bellicose Freydis is

---

[41] Not all scholars subscribe to this interpretation of the episode. See *Race* 266–269 on the range of readings proposed for this episode.

likely a foil for an idealized Gudrid, with both women lessoning us as to what women should, and should not, be for their societies.

Yet the episode staging two women from vastly different worlds – one Christian and representing the Latin West, the other presumably "pagan" and representing Native North America – who meet in the domestic setting of a woman's home, with an infant close by, memorably remains. I suggest the episode can be offered to students as a narrative attempt – of however limited or fleeting a kind – to imagine a bridge across difference.

We should not exaggerate the success of this narrative attempt, of course. For instance, no Native tongue or speech is ever heard – Gudrid's words only function as a kind of echo chamber, as the Indigenous woman repeats Gudrid's words back to her, trying out the Norse syllables on her tongue. The sudden conclusion to the episode, moreover, truncated by male violence rearing its head once again, also does not portend a happy outcome for Europe's encounters with Native North America.

But I work hard to find and help students see the *possibility* – even if it exists merely as a shadow, or a hint – of bridges across difference being imagined, perhaps as a thought experiment, within a text. While we aim to teach students critical thinking and incisive analysis that often require degrees of disenchantment, the production of an unremitting narrative of woe – unearthing a thousand years of othering, racism, exploitation, and domination in the textual record – can imbue in students a paralyzing, existential sense of dread and pessimism.

Finding moments like the episode between the two women, episodes which awaken curiosity and instigate discussion, then helps to interrupt, and ameliorate, any inadvertent production of an overarching, totalizing narrative that discourages, rather than encourages, idealism and action in the young.[42]

It is also important to point to the role played by *children* in the *Sagas*. Exhibits at the L'Anse aux Meadows heritage project, overseen by Parks Canada today, rightly call attention to the unique role of Snorri Thorfinnsson, Gudrid's infant and the first European child to be born in the Americas, so far as we know. But *ESR* also highlights *two Native American boys* who are abducted from their parents by the expeditioners, baptized, and taught language (i.e., Old Norse), and who then become native informants relaying ethnographic information that the saga duly narrates (102–103).

These kidnapped boys, students should be told, form an important historical-anthropological hinge, and not only in the way the saga relates. Scientists today

---

[42] I am indebted to Rachel Ooi, a student in my early global literature class at Yale-NUS College in Singapore, for teaching me this. I often find that I learn as much from students as they do from me, which underscores how much teaching experiments are really learning experiments for professors.

have discovered that Native Americans and Icelanders share DNA in the form of the C1e gene element: a genetic inheritance shared by no other ethnoracial groups in the world (*Race* 270–271). While scientists rightly do not expatiate on the meaning of this shared genetic heritage – beyond suggesting that unrecorded intermarriage might have occurred in premodernity – students can see, with this genetic evidence, the historicity of the *Sagas* in an immediate and forceful way.

Most importantly, we can call attention to the myriad ways the *Sagas* can be used to counter white supremacists who see the Vinland expeditions as an example of early European supremacy. For white supremacists, "Hail Vinland!" is a rallying cry today that has displaced "Heil Hitler," as supremacists imagine themselves as latter-day "Vikings" continuing an "ancient battle" in the Americas.[43] Students are tickled to learn that, contrary to white-supremacist wishful thinking, the *Vinland Sagas* depict Native American success, and European failure, as the would-be settler-colonists are routed from Vinland, and that thereafter, Native American genes spread to Iceland, complicating ideas of who has conquered whom.

Thanks to early encounters in North America, on which the *Vinland Sagas* open a window, white supremacists who are so proud of their white heritage are not even really as white as they think they are. This is something students discover when they take a course in early global literature.[44]

Teaching *Sundiata: An Epic of Old Mali*

To the question, "Where were the Black people in the Middle Ages?" the epic of Sunjata returns the panorama of a thriving, dynamic trans-Saharan Africa: a vast Black Africa alive in indigenous story traditions, visitor accounts by sojourners such as the world-traversing Moroccan Ibn Battuta, poetry, song, dance, performance arts, music, monuments, gold, sculptures, law codes, games, rituals, festivities, and treasure, among a plethora of expressive and material culture.

Students reading Sunjata,[45] the best-known of premodern African epics, learn that before there was a Wakanda in modern pop culture, there was the

---

[43] See, e.g., the neo-Nazi Jeremy Joseph Christian, who adapts Richard B. Spenser's "Hail Trump!" into "Hail Vinland!" (Wilson).

[44] Though I have little room to discuss them here, the modern-day texts, *Skraelings*, and *The Ice Hearts*, authored by writers of Indigenous heritage, offer alternative ways to imagine the early encounters between the Nordic settler-colonists and the Native populations of North America, with *Skraelings* in particular featuring the importance of a child. See Young and Mudan Finn for a discussion.

[45] Transliterated from Mande, the name Sundiata/Sunjata is variously spelled (Johnson's translation spells it as Son-Jara), as are those of many personages in the epic. I use *Sundiata* when referring to Kouyaté-Niane-Pickett's text, and "Sunjata" when referring to the character. Students should be told that in many premodern texts, personages can have more than one

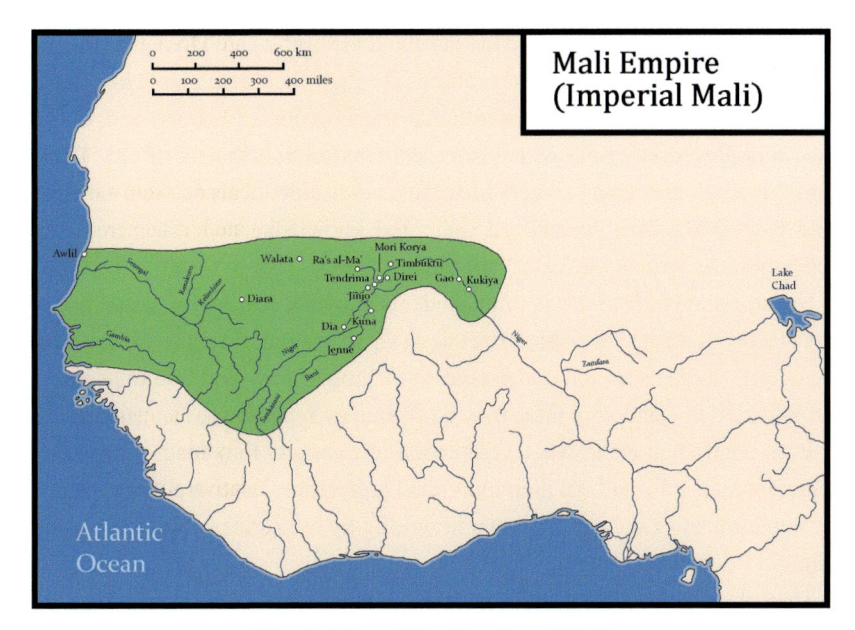

Fig. 1: Map of the Empire of Mali

massive premodern Empire of Mali, stretching at its height from the Atlantic Ocean to the interiors of central Africa, encompassing nearly half a million square miles (Gomez, *African Dominion* 220), preceded by the kingdoms of Ghana, and succeeded by the empire of Songhay (see Fig. 1).

Beyond West Africa, civilizations in Ethiopia, Nubia, the Swahili Coast, Zimbabwe, Benin, among others, have been excavated, studied, and offered to the academy and the public through books and articles, heritage sites, digital projects, and film and television documentaries that should, at their best, have made it unlikely, if not impossible, for questions like those addressed to Whitaker to be asked – yet knowledge of premodern Africa seems to have been siloed in ways that prevented it from reaching my colleague's otherwise "well-educated" interlocuters.

Sundiata can thus be offered to students as a gateway to the rich cultures and societies of premodern Africa across siloes of knowledge, with journeys of discovery made through student presentations and reports, term papers, and collaborative projects that students can be asked to undertake.[46]

---

name – e.g., Sunjata is also known as Mari Jata, among other sobriquets – and can also have various praise-names. Besides Mande, the epic is recounted in a number of African languages.

[46] In one striking student project, Jeffrey Fleisher at Rice University had his students build 3D houses at Songo Mnara on the Swahili coast, with technological assistance: http://virtualrecon struction.rice.edu/songomnara.html See also Kusimba's Element on the Swahili coast, and Binyam and Krebs' on Ethiopia. The G-MAP platform draws attention to the Timbuktu

Students are always impressed to read about the birth of an African empire, as recorded by its people over the centuries through their *griots* or *jeliw*: bard-archivists entrusted with the generational transmission of history, and whose ancestors played key roles as advisors and counselors to rulers of old. These bardic reciters-musicians-singers-historians-counselors descend from families who pass down their specialized, inherited knowledge and role across the generations as virtually a "caste" privilege.[47]

Unsurprisingly, *Sundiata* is often students' favorite text in my global literature classes. It is a text that should be taught with substantial contextualization at the outset. Students should understand something of how oral traditions transmit knowledge – and why there may be formulaic repetitions, inconsistencies, or even contradictions in whatever version of *Sundiata* they read, narrated by contemporary jeliw with all their individual preferences, after oral transmission for hundreds of years, and set down in writing by transcribers, translators, and editors.

They should also understand that numerous variants of the epic exist – by a 1997 count, there are sixty-four published versions (in addition to oral performances by living jeliw) – and the translation they read is but *one* version of the multi-variant epic of Old Mali, and other variants may offer details of plot and treatment differing greatly from the version they read, even when a core content exists (Gomez, *African Dominion* 390–392 n.2).[48]

These substantial caveats do not seem to deter instructors or students, however, and the epic is encountered in full or abridged form in many kinds of courses. Berkeley's ORIAS websites, designed for K-12 educators, testifies to the epic's enduring popularity: https://orias.berkeley.edu/resources-teachers/monomyth-heros-journey-project/sundiata

The texts listed in Section 4 are the most often used English translations of the epic in classroom teaching: the Longman's/Pearson's translation by D(jibril) T(amsir) Niane and G. D. Pickett, transposed and edited from the narration of Mamoudou Kouyaté, who claims descent in the lineage of the Kouyatés serving

---

manuscripts project, and the Zamani Project's multimillion-dollar initiatives of digitization, data collection, heritage preservation, and generational training in archeological expertise: http://www.globalmiddleages.org/content/external

[47] "Castes" in the Mande world, Johnson stresses (he finds at least four) function socioeconomically, as the right to pursue inherited occupations, and are not hierarchical "pecking orders," as they might be, e.g., in Hindu India (*Epic* 3).

[48] Gomez tells us the *songs* in the epic are the oldest materials, and to some extent constrain bardic improvision ("*Epic*" 149, *African Dominion* 64). *Griot* is from French, while *jeli* (sg.) and *jeliw* (pl.) are from the Mande/Mandinka languages of Manden (referring to the land, as well as the peoples of Mali, who are also known as Mande/Mandinka peoples). For their research presentations, some of my students have recreated jeli song performances, and reported on the lives and practices of jeliw today.

Sunjata's royal Keita line; the Hackett translation by David C. Conrad, transcribed from an abridged oral narration by Djanka Tassey Condé of the Condés of Fadama; and the Sisòkò-Johnson translation (*Epic*), performed by the jeli Fa-Digi Sisòkò, and recorded, transcribed, and translated in stages by an African-western team of six collaborators coordinated by John William Johnson.

My preference is to teach the Kouyaté-Niane-Pickett translation, "the most influential single version of the story" as base text, in part because it has the fullest rendition of the epic's key materials, while occasionally interleaving details from Condé-Conrad and Sisòkò-Johnson to discuss alternate traditions and story details (Belcher 92). Instructors who want to stress the performance aspects of contemporary oral narrations of the epic may prefer to center the Sisòkò-Johnson or Condé-Conrad translations instead.

The Condé-Conrad abridgement (which contains omissions of many passages that are summarized for readers by the translator) features a chatty jeli-narrator who intrudes modern musings ranging from his thoughts on race ("Americans are the best of the white people" [98]) to repeated mentions of muskets, guns, and gunpowder, that is, nonexistent technology in premodern Mali (e.g., 29, 55, 64, 69, 85, 92, 103, 109, 115, 119).[49] A colleague who has taught the Norton anthology extract excerpted from Condé-Conrad reports that students became confused by, and skeptical of the narrator – whose proclamations about cities ("if Paris was ever built by anyone, it was God"), musings on Black–White relations ("God made blackness after he made whiteness"), and views on women ("No matter how proud a girl is, once you call her 'beautiful,' she will soften") – are admittedly odd, to put it gently (100, 4, 23).

But the Condé-Conrad translation is highly interesting as a rendition of orality, featuring a jeli with a big personality and many opinions, responding to his audience in a lively, sprawling way – catering, for instance, to avid interest in family genealogies of not-necessarily-central characters who are ancestors (while omitting core events of the epic), and interpolating modern topics and his personal opinions to bring alive the dynamics of performance. Dramatizing how orature works, this translation would be excellent for courses on performance and the dramatic arts. It also offers engaging material for courses on medievalism.

Still, for those interested in oral performance as a dynamic process, even in a written text, the Sisòkò-Johnson translation is likely a better choice. This is a word-for-word transcription of a four-hour performance of the epic in verse (with rare prose interpolations by the translator) recited by a jeli whose cadences

---

[49] The Sisòkò-Johnson translation also has a Traore hunter shoot the buffalo-woman, Do Kamissa, with a gun: "He cleared the chamber of his gun,/And rammed some shot inside/And discharged the powder on the buffalo" (*Epic* 39).

are beautifully caught in the transcription – a jeli, moreover, who has an assistant-apprentice commenting on his recitation throughout, in a call-and-response dynamic well-captured in the text.[50] Much is opaque in the narration, however, and Johnson's copious notes are absolutely essential to study carefully, for students to make sense of what they are reading.

Delightfully, the jeli-narrator in Sisòkò-Johnson uses ideophones to convey actions, like making a tearing sound, "fèsè fèsè fèsè!" as Sunjata's dog rips Dankaran Tuman's dog to shreds (*Epic* 64), or a falling sound, "gejebu!" when Sogolon drops to her knees (*Epic* 61), and a rushing sound, "birri birri birri" as Susu people pursue Fakoli, and "yrrrrrrr!" when they attack him (*Epic* 61). The liveliness of the orature communicates a sense of immediacy, a sense of you-are-there, that is unmatched. This jeli-narrator contradicts himself or loses the thread when he is tired; he takes breaks, then forgets where he left off. For students of ethnography, folklore, anthropology, drama, orature, and performance arts, the Sisòkò-Johnson translation is superior.

Graduate students might forge a path through the copious notes more easily, to understand what's happening in the Sisòkò-Johnson narrative line-by-line, and a graduate class can usefully read Sisòkò-Johnson's fuller companion volume, *Son-Jara: The Mande Epic, Madekan/English Edition with Notes and Commentary* as base text. Indeed, if an instructor can afford to spend several weeks on Sunjata, a comparison of Sisòkò-Johnson, Condé-Conrad, and Kouyaté-Niane-Pickett would yield many fruitful discussions on the role of narrators and audiences, translations, and the retrieval of stories across time.

The Kouyaté-Niane-Pickett version (henceforth, *Sundiata*), is compact, yet highly detailed and vivacious, and a pragmatic choice that readily allows us to approach the diegesis as a set of key stories within a central epic framework – a narrative tree – from start to finish, by a griot who substantially refrains from foregrounding his personality, or indulging in digressions.[51] Students immediately recognize what narrative trees are like – acclimated as they are to contemporary popular culture, where narrative trees proliferate (e.g., the capacious *Star Trek* universe) – so that changes in details across alternate versions of stories tend to excite questions of *why*, which can prompt lively discussions.

Michael A. Gomez' recent scholarship guides us to see the epic as narrating the formation of an African empire out of earlier regional polities in the thirteenth century, while establishing the geographic boundaries and constituent territories of that empire at its most powerful expanse and greatest height in the

---

[50] The role of Bèmba, Sisòkò's *naamusayer* is "to give the bard encouragement," which can help the jeli develop an idea, change direction, or shape the narrative in other ways, as recitation proceeds (*Epic* 106 n.49).

[51] Page numbers I cite from the text refer to Kouyaté-Niane-Pickett's *Sundiata*.

fourteenth ("*Epic*;" *African Dominion*, chapters 5–7). Simultaneously, Gomez points to how Islam, a global religion, starts to take root among the Mande/Mandinka, embedding itself in social structures and spreading its influence.[52]

We thus see early globalism in West Africa taking the form of global religious forces that arrive, and negotiate local and regional cultures and societies, transforming political structures and human relations, personal identities, and producing new articulations of power.

Signs of Islam are everywhere in the epic. We learn that Sunjata's royal family, the Keitas, impressively claim descent from Bilal ibn Rabah, the Black African companion to the Prophet Mohammad, who occupies the esteemed role of the first muezzin or summoner of the faithful to prayer (2). Princes of Mali make the hajj (2). Sunjata wears the robes of "a great Muslim king," and Islamic jinn populate the narrative alongside indigenous deities (73, 70–72).

Traditional beliefs, practices, and forces do not disappear, however, but transact an intertwining coexistence with Islamic beliefs, practices, and forces; and scholars invariably point to the religious syncretism the epic exhibits. Animal sacrifices are made to Islamic forces like jinn, but also to indigenous deities; individuals may possess pre-Islamic occult forms of personal power (*nyama*, *dalilu*) that are inherited or achieved, but can also possess Islamic gifts of grace and blessings (*baraka*); and merchants who spread Islam jostle alongside the powerful old hunter-guilds and smiths of pre-Islamic society (*African Dominion* 91).

Revealingly, one outcome of globalism-as-religion is a transformation in leadership roles earlier occupied by women:

> [Older] Mande traditions . . . include . . . women who assume the *mansaya* or rulership, with accounts from the Gambia region asserting the very first *mansa* of Niumi was a woman, *Mansa* Mama Andame Jammeh, who was succeeded by another woman, *Mansa* Wame. Niumi in fact boasts twelve women who consecutively held the *mansaya*, while states all along the Gambia claim female rulers, from Baddibu to Wuli. Perhaps this was characteristic of Mande society (at least astride the Gambia) before Islam (*African Dominion* 71–72).

In the epic of Mali, however, Mande women are not rulers, but "become alternative sites of power" through "their resituation as sorcerers and reification as mothers" (*African Dominion* 74):

---

[52] This segment of Section 5 is guided by Gomez's scholarship; *African Dominion* has extensive notes and bibliographies that point to other translations/editions of the epic, and a large corpus of secondary literature.

> The ... close association between Sunjata and his mother, then between Sunjata and his sister, reflects the degree to which Sunjata is the product of women, not just in the biological sense, but also in the ideational realm, their spiritual abilities indispensable to Sunjata's survival and rise .... demonstrating Mande society's high regard for women while engendering spheres of power (political and spiritual) that plausibly reflect historical processes (*African Dominion* 74).[53]

Some of the totemic power of women is glimpsed in the story of the buffalo-woman of Do (Daw), Do Kamissa ("Kamissa of Daw"), who in her animal form as a wild buffalo ravages the countryside until she is killed by two Traore hunters whom she advises on how to kill her and ask for Sogolon Kedju, Sunjata's future mother, as their reward.

Sundiata only has a terse account of Kamissa's deeds, but other versions elaborate that she has been disenfranchised by her brother(s) from property rights because she is female, or that she has been mistreated by her nephew, the ruler of Do, who's her foster-son: Her rampaging then becomes a kind of feminine retribution for injustice (Condé-Conrad 28–29, Sisòkò-Johnson, *Epic* 31–33). Following the buffalo-woman's instructions, the hunters bring Sogolon to Maghan Kon Fatta (Maghan the Handsome), Sunjata's father-to-be, who has already received prophetic tidings that the hideously ugly woman he receives will birth a child who will be "the seventh conqueror of the earth," and "more mighty than Alexander" (6).[54]

Sogolon's hyperbolic ugliness is legion in all versions of the epic. In *Sundiata*, she has a hump, monstrous eyes, and bulbous breasts, her body covered in long hairs, like an animal (6–7, 11).

> If there is unanimity within the oral corpus ... it is that Sogolon Kedju – Sogolon Kèjugu, Souloulou-Koutouma, Sukulung Konte, Sira Nyading – is "monstrously ugly." One source calls her "Sogolon the Warty," with seven large, distinct bodily protuberances, having one eye higher than the other, one leg longer than the other, one arm shorter than the other, and one buttock larger than the other. Another calls her "Sukulung the Spotty," covered with pockmarks, while yet another says she has three hundred breasts and three

---

[53] Gomez suggests that "[t]he most popular interpretation is that 'Sunjata' conjoins 'Sogolon' and 'Jata' (signifying 'Sogolon's lion')" – an interpretation highlighting the hero's tie to his mother (*African Dominion* 75). *Sundiata* underscores that importance: "the child is worth no more than the mother is worth" (22). Given that "the lion is the totem and ancestor of the Keitas" students might like to think about whether Sunjata, the lion who founds an empire, is the original Lion King (*Sundiata* 85 n.2).

[54] Alexander the Great is mentioned several times in *Sundiata*. Students can be asked to notice how, as a legendary force of globalism, Alexander (or Iskandar Zulkarnain, his Islamic incarnation) recurs in the semester's texts to confer globality, antiquity, and prestige on royal lineages.

hundred humps. She is otherwise described as a hairless "hunchback," in mimicry of a buffalo (*African Dominion* 72).[55]

While jeliw no doubt enjoy teasing out Sogolon's ugliness, students are often struck by how the monstrosity of the bride, juxtaposed against the handsomeness of the groom, reverses the familiar Beauty-and-the-Beast story-formula of the West. If the Beast, in this African epic, is the woman, and Beauty is the man, what does that say about the values of this African society?

They soon see that with the birth of Sunjata, mention of Sogolon's hideousness fades, and her exemplarity as a mother becomes the focus instead. The story thus suggests that it is *female fertility, not female beauty*, that matters most. Sogolon gains in status and importance once maternity is achieved: Motherhood, and the birth of important sons, confers status and authority in premodern texts.

But in order for Sogolon to conceive Sunjata, a struggle must first take place between her very strong "wraith" and Maghan Keita's, as Beauty repeatedly fails to impregnate the Beast on their wedding night and continues to fail for a week (11–12). Presented as combat, a male-female struggle is shown to occur between occult powers possessed by the woman, and occult powers possessed by the man – which might be a way to affirm the groom's aversion to the bride's looks, perhaps, or the near-universal preference of virgins in epic stories not to be deflowered – to explain why the king cannot perform:

> Naré Maghan tried to perform his duty as a husband but Sogolon repulsed his advances. He persisted, but his efforts were in vain and early the next morning Doua [his griot] found the king exhausted, like a man who had suffered a great defeat. "I have been unable to possess her – and besides, she frightens me, this young girl . . . . when I drew close to her during the night her body became covered with long hairs and that scared me very much. All night long I called upon my wraith but he was unable to master Sogolon's" (11).

This allegorical struggle between the sexes ends when the king frightens his bride with a lie, she faints, and he impregnates her. *Sundiata* draws a veil over the impregnation, yet students are never in doubt that the reason Sogolon wakes up "already a wife," and having conceived Sunjata, is that a rape occurred while she was unconscious (12). If you ask students why, in their opinion, there's

---

[55] In some versions, Do Kamissa is Sogolon's aunt – gesturing to a web of family relations that helps to naturalize motives and behavior – and Sogolon's resemblance to the buffalo-woman is thus made more obvious. Some versions explain Kamissa's willingness to reveal the secret of how to kill her buffalo-form as a reward for the hunters' charity, or because she succumbs to a hex secreted in food the hunters offer her, or that she simply realizes her time has come. Students usually recognize that encounters with an old woman/hag who has a message and/or secret to deliver, and who proffers help, are a time-honored story motif.

a rape, and obstacles to the birth of this hero – and the less-than-moral circumstances surrounding the birth of other heroes in other epics and romances –
a lively classroom discussion will ensue that can later be picked up in other
texts, including *The Secret History of the Mongols*.[56]

Sogolon's disabling ugliness, and Sunjata's childhood years of crawling
around on all fours before (instigated by his mother) he finally hauls himself
up and decides to walk through a massive act of will, then afford an opportunity
to discuss the role of disability in the epic.[57] To explain why Sunjata doesn't
walk till he is seven years old (or seventeen, or older, in variants), the story has it
that he is either a lazy, lax, and greedy child, or that Naré Maghan's first wife
Sassuma Berete hamstrings the child with a hex, or something else (15, 18;
Condé-Conrad 49).

"Many sources present this as a disability (as opposed to volition)," Gomez
says, "maintaining that he was either born in this condition or becomes
a 'cripple' later in childhood. Whether congenital or subsequent, it becomes
a site of miraculous transformation and verification of divine destiny" (*African
Dominion* 75).

That disability can be the sign of a divine destiny, and destiny can be
immanent in an ugly woman, are important ideas the epic attests. Indeed,
Johnson points out that in premodern Mali "Deformed people, or those with
epilepsy, are considered by many to be possessed of special occult power
(*nyama*). Presumably such a person would be of benefit [to society] because
of his/her power" (Sisòkò-Johnson, *Epic* 113). Story traditions foregrounding
alternative ideas about deformity, beauty, and disability may be one reason the
epic of Mali is a favorite text of students.

Ultimately, however, Gomez suggests,

> The Do-Kamissa-cum-Sogolon-Kedju saga … serves dual, seemingly
> contradictory purposes: it affirms the righteous indignation of women over
> the loss of political power, yet it celebrates the political sphere as the preserve
> of men – as Sunjata was, after all, a man. In this way, the account of Sunjata's
> circumstances is a mechanism of assuagement and legitimization, a double
> move, responding to women's resentment through their resituation as sor-
> cerers and reification as mothers (*African Dominion* 73–74).

The epic of Old Mali is not alone or unique, of course, in its portrayal of "good"
women as those who serve the interests of male protagonists, while "evil" women
are those who supposedly cause communal vulnerability and destruction because

---

[56] A trigger warning is helpful: Needless to say, discussing rape, even in a centuries-old story, can
re-evoke personal trauma.
[57] I owe the thought here to Chris Baswell, who teaches *Sundiata* as part of courses on disability.

of their ambitions. The *Vinland Sagas* have Gudrid/Freydis, and the epic of Mali has Sogolon/Sassuma, rival co-wives of Maghan Keita.

But *Sundiata* is arguably unusual for *the extent* to which the epic acknowledges that the hero's success depends on women. In his decisive epic battles, Sunjata finds that his principal foe, the sorcerer-king Sumaoro Kanté of the Susu people, wields a powerful occult magic that even Sunjata, with all his *nyama*, *dalilu*, and *baraka*, his sacrifices to jinn and deities, military prowess, and strategic confederation of West Africa's forces, cannot overcome.[58]

Iron weapons bounce off Sumaoro, who can also vanish at will, making him impossible to defeat in the battlefield through the usual means of war (52). "Didn't people say that Sumaoro could assume sixty-nine different shapes to escape his enemies?" the narrator asks, "to beat the king of Sosso other weapons were necessary" (52).[59]

Sumaoro's sole weakness, it turns out, is that he is magically vulnerable to a white rooster's spur – a secret that Nana Triban, Sunjata's half-sister who's the daughter of Sassuma (or, in some versions, Kolonkan, Sunjata's full-sister by Sogolon), ferrets out of Sumaoro, when she becomes one of the sorcerer-king's wives or concubines, and flatters him into an unwary bedchamber disclosure (*Sundiata* 57–58, 64).[60]

Armed with this powerful knowledge, Sunjata merely has to graze Sumaoro with a white rooster's spur, and "Sumaoro felt his powers leave him" (65). Sorcery and a woman's cunning win the battle, and the defeat of this formidable foe is what allows Sunjata to reclaim his homeland, recover the territories ravaged by Sumaoro, and unite regional polities into the new Empire of Mali.[61]

The revelation of a woman's crucial agency in securing the genesis of the Malian empire is, like all that Gomez notices, a double-edged moment, "key in what is otherwise a masculinist enterprise, her intervention a critique of that

---

[58] Pre-battle, *Sundiata* depicts an exchange of taunts and boasts between Sunjata and Sumaoro, wonderfully conducted by proxy via the leaders' messenger *owls*. While pre-battle boasts and taunts are a staple of epic, students are delighted by the talking owls who ventriloquize the robust back-and-forth exchange, often wondering if J. K. Rowling had stolen the idea from the epic of Mali for her Harry Potter series (60–61). Sisòkò-Johnson has Sunjata sending a partridge to Sumaoro to deliver his message (*Epic* 89).

[59] In Sisòkò-Johnson, Sumaoro's praise-name "the King of Yesteryear" (*Epic* 69) emphasizes "a pagan versus Moslem theme in the epic, with Son-Jara representing the [new] Moslem forces. Some have suggested this theme as the key to understanding the real meaning of the epic" (*Son-Jara* 288–289 n.1825).

[60] Whether she is a plucky volunteer or sent by force to be Sumaoro's wife (57), her sexual agency or victimhood is seen as a sacrifice she makes for her brother's cause (*African Dominion* 83).

[61] "The importance of the magical element in the conflict can hardly be over-stated; this runs counter to the battle orientation of much European epic .... [T]he real conflict takes place on the level of occult power; once that is settled, the battle is something of a foregone conclusion" (Belcher 104).

masculinity" (*African Dominion* 83).[62] That a woman secures victory on the battlefield with a bedroom secret is a way to say that men ultimately depend on women, but it is also a cautionary tale to say men should also fear women for their wiles and bedroom treachery, a caution as old as the tale of the Nazirite Samson.

Attributions of female agency and responsibility occur in major and minor key in the epic's variants. In Sisòkò-Johnson, Sunjata's family has a famed *female* griot or *jelimuso*, Tumu Maniya, who announces Sunjata's birth to his father before Sassuma's messenger is able to announce Sassuma's son's birth, thereby formally establishing Sunjata as the ruler's first-born son (*Epic* 49–51). This jelimuso (and not Sunjata's jeli, Balla Faséké, in *Sundiata*) sings the praise-song, the "Song of the Bow," when Sunjata finally stands up and starts to walk – and Sunjata walks not because of bending an iron rod made by male smiths into a bow, as in *Sundiata*, but because of a staff *his mother* cut for him from a custard apple tree (*Epic* 57–60, 62).[63] Tumu Maniya is the creator of the iron rasp, a hunter's musical instrument; accompanies Sunjata's family into exile; and is prominent in announcing events.

The hero's return to Mali from exile is also accomplished through a woman, Sunjata's sister Kolonkan. In *Sundiata*, after exilic wandering that maps the boundaries of the Malian empire-to-be, and future political relations between Sunjata and his tributary companion-chiefs, Sogolon's small refugee family arrives in Mema, where Sunjata grows to adulthood and rises in palace leadership over time. In due course, a group from Manden/Mali arrives, looking for Sunjata's help against Sumaoro, and posing as merchants in the marketplace selling condiments harvested from Malian native plants.

A touching scene of reconciliation occurs when Kolonkan, shopping in the market, recognizes baobab and gnougou, plants which used to grow in her mother's garden, and delightedly brings the visitors back to her mother. Joy poignantly ensues as "Sogolon took the baobab leaves and gnougou in her hand

---

[62] Condé-Conrad lacks this sororal intervention that Gomez calls "consistent with a pattern of female rescue in Sunjata's life" (*African Dominion* 83). Sisòkò-Johnson has Kolonkan offer herself to Sumaoro, and return with Sumaoro's three secrets (*Epic* 91-93).

[63] "Often, in available recorded versions, the griot who accompanies Sunjata early in his travels is not Bala Faseke, but a woman, Tumu Maniya, and it is she who composes and sings the 'Song of the Bow'," "perhaps the best-known song associated with Sunjata" (Belcher 109, 99). "In many versions, he raises himself on a staff cut by his mother ... or he leans on her shoulder, or even on the walls of her hut .... His rising is the subject of great rejoicing, and his mother sings a variety of songs expressing her pride and delight" (Belcher 97). "Some versions of the story thus make this a festive women's moment .... The lyric material (some of Sunjata's forty praise songs) seems particularly designed for delivery by women. Whether this might imply an intended audience of women as well is impossible to determine, but the notion seems plausible" (Belcher 98–99).

and put her nose to them as though to inhale all the scent," "turning the precious condiments over and over in her hands" (44). This moving moment, in which sister and mother play prominent roles, marks the beginning of Sunjata's return from exile and subsequent confronting of Sumaoro (43–45).[64]

This episode also foregrounds the importance of *merchants* in premodern societies. Sogolon and her small family of refugees joined merchant caravans in their exilic wandering to ensure safe travel, and "the merchants were good to Sogolon and her children" (32). The refugees are also recognized as Manden's royal family by an embassy posing as merchants. Merchants, of course, are the arterial conduits of the premodern world, bringing news to far-flung societies separated by great distances, offering protection to traveling pilgrims or diplomats or refugees, and they stitch together the thriving commercial networks of the premodern world. In accounts where merchants are not themselves the protagonists, it's helpful for students to notice the presence of merchants as facilitators in narrative webs.

Merchants' goods, like baobab and gnougou, also point students to the many interlacing layers of material culture in Manden society. It's significant that *crops* are the means by which social recognition and conciliation occur, testifying to the importance of plant domesticates. In each text, students can be asked to notice what plants and animals are important to a society, what items of material culture matter, and what constitutes abundance, or affords prestige, in that society.

Plants and animals are highlighted everywhere in *Sundiata*. The nine great witches of Mali whom Sassuma sets on Sunjata are moved by Sunjata's generosity when he urges them to take what they want from his mother's garden – loading them with aubergines, onions, and gnougou – when he catches them stealing her vegetables. He also betters the reward Sassuma promises them (cows, calves, rice, and hay) by giving them bushmeat: nine of the twelve elephants he has killed, one for each of them (24–26).

---

[64] Condé-Conrad substitutes instead a gendered quarrel between Kolonkan and Manding Bori (Sunjata's half-brother and closest companion). Manding Bori is offended by Kolonkan's removal by magic of the internal organs of deer he and Sunjata have killed: "Does she have to prove her female powers to us? I won't spare her when I see her in town; she'll soon know that I wear the pants in this family" (83–84). "Manden Bori tripped Ma Kolonkan and threw her down. Her wrapper came loose" (85). Kolonkan is furious at being exposed naked before the visitors – "You've shamed me in front of the Mande people. Shamed me!" – and curses her half-brother's descendants (85). Kolonkan's earlier happiness at the visitors' arrival is also glossed differently: "She was happy because she knew that the visitors from Manden would not leave her behind. She had long since reached the age of marriage, and she knew she'd be married when she returned to Manden" (83). By contrast, Sisòkò-Johnson sympathetically portrays Kolonkan's actions as a hostess's concern to feed the Malian visitors the best parts of the kill – the animals' internal organs – and the jeli-narrator chivalrously shields Kolonkan from voyeurism by saying she's still clothed by her slip, even as her "skirts" fell off (*Epic* 81–84).

We see rulers like Maghan Keita distributing gifts of grain, clothes, gold, and fine loincloths, as well as large quantities of rice during celebrations (10–11, 14). This is a society where women wear gold in their hair, their wrists heavy with silver bracelets (9). Medicinal leaves are used to heal wounds and cure diseases (3), and the importance of sacrificial animals such as red bulls, white bulls, white rams, and white roosters is everywhere stressed (6, 50, 56, 71, 79). This is also a society where musical instruments like the balafon (see Fig. 2), strings, and tam-tams are important, alongside song and dance, and where iron tools and weapons – such as Sunjata's bow, that only he could bend, like Odysseus' – do not fail to be mentioned (10, 13, 21, 37).

Material and expressive culture show Manden to be a courtly and warrior society. Feasting, ritual celebrations, spectacles, and festivities abound. A hundred smiths in the royal forges of Manden manufacture bows, spears, arrows, and shields for warriors. Rich carpets, fine scimitars, and splendid weapons ornament the halls of kings in West Africa, who like to play games of wit and skill (20, 30, 34). Horses are prized, underscoring the importance of cavalry as well as infantry in war: The victorious Sunjata is greeted by the women of Mali who lay down their colorful wrappers, so that his horse need not dirty its hooves (80).

Fig. 2: The balafon, a griot's musical instrument

Hospitality to travelers and strangers is another important theme in premodern global texts, foregrounded by the degrees of hospitality Sogolon and her family receive in their epic journey into exile. Without being able to depend on the hospitality of others, including strangers, premodern travel would largely have been impossible.

Most importantly, the epic of Mali attests the dictum that, for the inhabitants of the world, every place is the center of the world. It tells us: If you want salt, go to Niani, the capital of Mali; if you want gold, go to Niani; if you want fine cloth, go to Niani; if you want fish, go to Niani; if you want meat, go to Niani; if you want to see an army, go to Niani; if you want to see a great king, go to Niani (82).

Sunjata, the "hero of many names," peerless among men, is lord of Niani, the center of the world. And because of he who gave the world peace, "Niani became the navel of the earth" (82).

Teaching Ibn Fadlan's *Mission to the Volga/Journey to Russia*

If the *Vinland Sagas* show resource extraction as a compelling motive for crossing an ocean, and *Sundiata* shows an African royal family traveling great distances because they are political refugees, the mission of Ahmad ibn Fadlan ibn al-Abbas ibn Rashid ibn Hammad – a representative from the tenth-century Abbasid empire – points to another reason for long-distance journeying: diplomacy.

Ibn Fadlan is an envoy or messenger (*rasul*) from the Caliph al-Muqtadir to Yiltawar, King of the Volga Bulghars (*Saqalibah*). The Bulghar king, a convert to Islam, has asked the Caliph for instruction in the faith, resources to build a mosque with a minbar from which the Caliph's name may be pronounced in Friday prayers, and a fort "to protect [Yiltawar] against the kings who opposed him" (3).[65]

Granting Yiltawar's requests allows al-Muqtadir to accomplish key goals in early globalism. Baghdad, center of the Abbasid Caliphate (but with rival caliphates in Iberia and North Africa), gets to acknowledge a Muslim kingdom at the peripheries of Islam's reach, and graciously send jurists and instructors as an act of doctrinal largesse that underscores Baghdad's religio-political centrality. Bonds are strengthened between center and periphery, and the empire's power and prestige are officially acknowledged in far-flung terrains.

At the same, the building of a fort in Bulghar territory not only secures the Bulghar king a military buttress against his neighboring rivals (chief of whom are the Khazars, whose king and elites have converted to a rival religion,

---

[65] Page numbers refer to James E. Montgomery's translation, but I interleave Frye's for its helpful ethnographic appendices and commentary.

Judaism), but helps to protect the lucrative trade in furs and slaves from the region for the Abbasids, a trade highly beneficial to Baghdad (xxxi–xxxii). Religion, commerce, and military-political goals thus dovetail in one diplomatic maneuver: an early version of the *mission civilisatrice*, so to speak, in fortuitous answer to the invitation of a regional power.

Ibn Fadlan – who is not the ambassador, but the man delegated to read the Caliph's letter to Yiltawar, supervise the requested jurists and instructors, and deliver the gifts from al-Muqtadir to the Bulghar king – ends up gifting later ages with a lively eyewitness account (henceforth, *Mission*) of his group's voyage from Baghdad, across Central Asia, and northward up the Volga, offering a vista of riches mined by scholars for information about the tenth-century worlds of Eurasia and its peoples, especially the Oghuz (or *Ghuzziyyah*, a seminomadic Turkic people who in the following century would issue forth into the Near East and become known as the Seljuks), the Bulghars (a Finno-Ugrian people later associated with the Volga Tatars), the Rus ("Russian Vikings"/"Northmen"), and the Khazars.

For students, Ibn Fadlan's account positions a *second* window into the international fur trade first glimpsed in the barter with Indigenous peoples, and Karlsefni's liquidation of his loot in Norway, in the *Vinland Sagas*. Here, we see merchants in Eurasia trading in sable and black fox, and the Bulghar king paying tribute to the Khazar king in sables – one for every tent in his kingdom (28, 31). We see that, like precious fabrics, furs are both export goods and international currency. Here, too, students are granted a second view of Nordic peoples, this time as the Rus (*Rusiyyah*), and described not by the Nordics themselves, but by someone from an Arab civilization rendered as infinitely more advanced and sophisticated.[66]

Students also encounter eyewitness testimony in global literature and can reflect on the apparent authority of first-person "reports" – which they will encounter again and again, including Marco Polo's – and how the narrator-witness's persona colors the narrative.[67] *This* particular narrator, students quickly see, complicates received notions of Orientalism encountered in modern literature classes where Edward Said, or Saidian-style criticism, is on the syllabus.

---

[66] A fruitful prompt is to ask students to extrapolate what tenth-century Abbasid society appears like, based on Ibn Fadlan's reactions to all he encounters. Their impressions can then be tested against what they find when they read Arabic texts in the syllabus or begin research for presentations and papers.

[67] Students should learn, of course, that the *author* of a premodern narrative can differ from *who writes down* the narrative – perhaps a scribe, or in the case of Ibn Fadlan's account, also Yaqut ibn Abdullah al-Rumi al-Hamawi, who quotes Ibn Fadlan extensively in his geographical dictionary (xxxiv–xxxv).

After all, Ibn Fadlan is a rapporteur *from the East*, so-called, who gazes upon the peoples of Central Asia and Eurasia in ways that Saidian discourse argues the West, so-called, gazes on the non-West, especially the East, constructing whole regions and peoples in projects of knowledge/power.[68] The examples here are numerous. Of the Khwarazmians, Ibn Fadlan says, "When they talk they sound just like starlings" (7). The speech of foreigners never sounds quite human, does it?

Another people, the Oghuz, "transhumant nomads" who live "wretched lives," "do not base their beliefs on reason," but decide matters "by consultation," and respect "the lowliest and most worthless individual in their community" – a process so demotic it seems ludicrous to the narrator (10). Oghuz are also unhygienic: They "do not clean themselves when they defecate or urinate," and "do not wash themselves when intercourse puts them in a state of ritual impurity" (10). Women are neither veiled nor secluded: "their womenfolk do not cover themselves in the presence of a man," and one man's wife even "uncovered her vulva and scratched it, right in front of us" (10).

Such racializing superciliousness, James E. Montgomery opines, is because "the imperial experience is at the heart of Ibn Fadlan's account" (xxv). Baghdad, where the Arboreal Mansion of al-Muqtadir had a silver-and-gold tree with swaying branches and singing birds, automata shaped as knights on horseback performing cavalry maneuvers, a famed menagerie with a lion house and elephant enclosure, and a caliphal complex boasting opulent architecture (xxvii) – the reasoning goes – makes the world Ibn Fadlan encounters elsewhere seem primitive to him.

But *Mission* also offers prime examples of how a representative from a *sedentary* civilization views peoples from *nomad* or *seminomadic* civilizations. If your syllabus includes John of Plano Carpini's *Historia Mongalorum*, and/or William of Rubruck's *Itinerarium*, here is an opportunity to ask students to consider similarities and contrasts in how a Muslim envoy from the Abbasid Empire, and a Franciscan envoy or missionary from the Latin West, views the nomadic/semi-nomadic peoples of Eurasia.

Students can be shown how a water taboo in continental Eurasia, issuing from exigent environmental circumstances, is moralized as filth and a lack of hygiene by an unsympathetic urbanite, and how the doctrinally prim can moralize variant bodily behaviors in other cultures as impious, or abhorrently immodest. This is also an opportunity to discuss the adaptive resourcefulness and range of

---

[68] *Mission* is also an excellent text with which to begin a discussion on the sheer adventitiousness of how cardinal and ordinal points are named, in the past and today – in a spherical world where the identification of geographic location by cardinal points is entirely relational and determined by investments of geopolitical and geocultural power.

human responses that have made for survival in difficult environmental conditions.

A graduate student, Patrick Naeve, once made the excellent point in class that the region of Eurasia Ibn Fadlan encounters must seem to him like a spatialized, geographic version of *jahiliyyah* – the time of ignorance, before the advent of Islam. Like a tenth-century panorama of the Wild, Wild West, this "place-time of ignorance" (Naeve) is both fascinating and shocking, a locale where anything can happen: where blood feuds, rough violence, and alien ways predominate, and myriad polities are jostling for power, far from the Abbasid center.

We might add that when Ibn Fadlan tutors the Bulghars on correct doctrinal practice in Islam (al-Muqtadir's instructors never make it, so Ibn Fadlan acts in their place), he speaks from the Shafii jurisprudential school of Islam dominant in Baghdad, opposing the Hanafi-based Islam of the Bulghars, and, through his admonishments, and stern attempts at correction, practices an evolutionary discourse of religious superiority.

A diplomat from the Near East, here, denies the world of Eurasia coevalness in myriad ways that students familiar with Johannes Fabian's *Time and the Other* will recognize, when other cultures are perceived as primitive and non-coeval with your own: located in backward eras of time that your own culture has long left behind, in its accomplishment of civilizational maturity. What is largely implicit in the *Vinland Sagas'* descriptions of Indigenous fascination with European metal weaponry is made explicit here: Ibn Fadlan's racializing discourse, like the *Sagas'*, pivots on the denial of coevalness to other societies.

Moreover, an example of a lookingglass, reverse Orientalism – Occidentalism? – occurs when Ibn Fadlan describes the Northmen known as the Rus, detailing the barbarous filth of these Nordics with eloquent disgust: "They are the filthiest of all God's creatures," "defecating or urinating and do not wash themselves when intercourse puts them in a state of ritual impurity" (33). "They have intercourse in full view of their companions. Sometimes they gather in a group and do this in front of each other" (33). The narrator saves the worst for last, in a portrayal vividly brought to life in the film *The Thirteenth Warrior*, a cinematic rendition of Michael Crichton's historical fantasy, *Eaters of the Dead*:

> They must wash their faces and their heads each day with the filthiest and most polluted water you can imagine .... Every morning a female slave brings a large basin full of water and hands it to her master. He washes his hands, face, and hair in the water. Then he dips the comb in the water and combs his hair. Then he blows his nose and spits in the basin. He is prepared to do any filthy, impure act in the water. When he has finished, the female slave carries the basin to the man next to him who performs the same routine

as his comrade. She carries it from one man to the next and goes around to everyone in the house. Every man blows his nose and spits in the basin, and then washes his face and hair (33).

The Rus – ethnic cousins to the *Vinland Sagas'* Greenlanders and Icelanders – are thus subjected to tenth-century Orientalism by a representative from what Said would consider the East.

What happens, then, to a concept like Orientalism, when "westerners" or "northerners" are described in Orientalist terms by an "easterner"? Or when Orientalism operates for the religiously devout as a category of pre-Islamic time, as *jahiliyyah*? Can there be Orientalism without an Orient, like racism before race, or nationalism before the existence of nations? Is Occidentalism reversed Orientalism?

Such questions repeatedly arise, when students read early global literatures alongside the modern literatures that are the standard fare of literature departments, reshaping their understanding of modern critical theory.

Delightfully, Ibn Fadlan's account also depicts the denigrated natives answering back to the representative of empire. When the narrator exclaims at the immodesty of Oghuz women, the husband of the woman who is comfortably scratching herself rejoins: "we might uncover it in your presence and you might see it, but she keeps it safe so that no one can get to it. This is better than her covering it up and letting others have access to it." Gamely, Ibn Fadlan admits: "Illicit intercourse is unheard of" among the Oghuz (11).

Similarly, as he witnesses a deceased Rus chieftain being cremated, he reports an unflattering view of Muslim funerary customs when one of the *Rusiyyah* dubs Arabs "a lot of fools" because "you ... take your nearest and dearest and those whom you hold in the highest esteem and put them in the ground, where they are eaten by vermin and worms. We ... cremate them there and then, so that they enter [heaven] on the spot" (38). Ibn Fadlan does not quite say the man has a point, but unexpectedly, a moment of religious comparatism materializes.

Indeed, it is the narrator's willingness to report *what the other thinks and says* – not merely limiting us to his own views alone – which hatches open moments where bridges across vast cultural divides can appear. One of these instants occurs right after Ibn Fadlan describes the unhygienic Oghuz: "One of them heard me reciting the Qur'an and found it beautiful. He approached the interpreter and said, 'Tell him not to stop'" (11).

Suddenly, our sense of these supposedly self-polluting, uncivilized Turks shifts in a breath: They are moved by aural beauty, which they value in the recitation of a sacred text alien to them, a deeply humanizing moment.

Likewise, the otherness of climate and atmospheric conditions in the north – a cold so extreme that the narrator reports they were all ready to die (9) – does not prevent Ibn Fadlan from marveling at other alien atmospheric conditions, such as the aurora borealis. A moment of cultural rapprochement crystallizes when he and Yiltawar agree on how to interpret the swirling red northern lights, and decide that the "men, animals, and weapons" they see in the sky are warring "groups of jinn, believers and unbelievers, who do battle" nightly (23).

Their shared wonder at the magnificent spectacle is tempered by our recognition that both come from military societies, so they reflexively see war and violence in the skies, rather than something more peaceably benign. But moments of connection between cultures, and appreciation rather than fear of the utterly alien, are not so common in literatures of encounter that we should fail to take opportunities to recognize and discuss them with students whenever we can.

For these and other reasons, *Mission* is a rewarding text to teach. Students who are following the trail of how women are portrayed in early global literatures will notice that in the Nordic funerary rites, it is an old woman, dubbed the "Angel of Death," who summons, prepares, stabs, and ensures the rape, torture, and death of the young female slave who is sacrificed to join her deceased master in the afterlife (35–37, Frye 68–70). They will remember that today, too, old women are usually the members of society who perform rites such as genital cutting on girls and young women, and can be asked to ponder how women are socialized, in the past and today, to accept and reproduce their roles.

Mission to the Volga also offers thick-descriptive details of what caravan routes and overland journeys are like: descriptions useful to compare across texts, and with depictions of sea journeys. Ibn Fadlan's embassy from Baghdad, like Sunjata's royal family, travels with merchants for safety – here, in a large caravan of 300 mounts and 5,000 men, covering on average ten miles a day (13). We see that in Eurasia fabric is the currency of choice, and gifts are expected by those they meet (which John of Plano Carpini, unable to grasp local economics, will moralize as greed, three centuries later). We also see that slaves are ubiquitous in the world, with soldier-slaves accompanying the Baghdad embassy, and women slaves ostensibly choosing death alongside their deceased Nordic masters.

Students will encounter variations of all this, again and again, across the texts of the semester.

6 Encountering the Other, or Slaves, Race, Religion, Gender, and Sexuality in a World of Differences: Teaching "The Slave of MS. H.6," selected documents from *India Traders of the Middle Ages*, Amitav Ghosh's *In an Antique Land: History in the Guise of a Traveler's Tale,* and Kamaluddin Abdul-Razzaq Samarqandi's *Mission to Calicut and Vijayanagar*

Teaching a text about the founding of an African empire, or about an embassy from an Islamic empire, or even the *Secret History of the Mongols*, raises an important question I have been asked: *How do we prevent the teaching of premodern global literatures from turning into a literary history of empires?*

After all, the texts descending to us are rarely, if ever, written by underclass authors about underclass communities, and those who want to teach histories-from-below face the dilemma that subaltern voices do not generously populate premodernity's archives. Even more for premodern than for modern societies, the documents that survive tend to be authored or authorized by society's elites.

Fortuitously, however, we have a cluster of texts utterly unconcerned with empires, and intently concerned with a slave, a merchant, and *fellaheen*: Amitav Ghosh's *Subaltern Studies* essay, "The Slave of MS. H. 6" (henceforth "Slave"); documents involving the India trader Abraham ben Yiju, lodged in the Genizah archive (Goitein and Friedman 594–605); and Ghosh's *In an Antique Land*, an account of his PhD fieldwork in Egypt, intercut by episodes Ghosh plausibly imagines from the twelfth-century India trader Abraham's life.[69] Serendipitously, these texts offer glimpses into what the life of an enslaved person in premodernity, from South Asia, might be like.

But first, a caveat. Premodern slavery is a complex subject, with a rapidly accumulating body of scholarship, and I've cautioned in various contexts that, depending on the archive, a focus on premodern slavery may end up less an exercise in understanding the microhistories of subaltern peoples – which the unwary might assume – than an exercise in seeing how enslavement in premodernity can lead to great power and position, as some of the enslaved rise to astonishing heights – becoming sultans, emirs, generals, admirals, viziers, ambassadors, queens, and regents – in Islamicate societies, Africa, and the many Asias.

It is important to acknowledge, therefore, that studying premodern slavery may ironically become yet another exercise in studying elites and empires. But it is equally important to begin *somewhere*. If we want students to grasp how premodern slavery differs from modern chattel slavery and contemporary human trafficking and unfreedoms, early global literatures offer excellent crucibles for scrutiny.

---

[69] For more on Abraham's life, see Lambourn; on the Malabar coast, Prange.

Teaching "The Slave of MS. H.6," selected documents from *India Traders of the Middle Ages,* and Amitav Ghosh's *In an Antique Land: History in the Guise of a Traveler's Tale*

In an Antique Land (henceforth, *AL*) is a much-read, highly-popular ethno-graphic-cum-historical narrative by the master-novelist Amitav Ghosh, while "Slave" is Ghosh's less-read, masterly exercise of historical scholarship. Both detail the writer's discovery of the existence of an enslaved man from India's Malabar coast, mentioned in letters written to Abraham ben Yiju by his friend and business associate Khalaf ibn Isaac, and lodged in the Genizah archive of documents.[70]

Identified in Judeo-Arabic by three consonants, B-M-H, this enslaved indi-vidual so haunts Ghosh that he teaches himself twelfth-century Judeo-Arabic paleography, and commits to intensive research to retrieve from the anonymity of history a possible name and identity, and the lineaments of a possible life lived by a single subaltern subject.

Antique Land's companion text, "Slave," is a rich exercise in historical scholarship: thorough, self-conscious, and thoughtful in acknowledging what it is able and unable to know. Ghosh learns that premodern slavery differs significantly from the Atlantic slavery of the plantation eras, and Abraham's man, far from being abject, is the trader's trusted "business agent, a respected member of his household" who accompanies maritime cargoes between Egypt and the Malabar coast ("Slave" 162):

> in many parts of the world, including Egypt and north India, slavery was the principal means of recruitment to positions of power in the state .... [I]n medieval India and in the Middle East, as in many African societies, slavery appears to have been a means of creating ties of fictive kinship ("Slave" 195–196)[71]

While the above is a condensed simplification, students may remember that Tyrkir, the enslaved "southerner" in *Greenlanders' Saga* who was part of Leif Eiriksson's household since Leif was a child, and who discovers wild grapes in Vinland and delivers his news in excited German, is welcomed with relief when

---

[70] The genizah of the Synagogue of the Palestinians in Old Cairo/Fustat – an attached chamber where miscellaneous documents bearing the name of God were kept until they could be respectfully disposed of – was never emptied, thus bequeathing the modern world a treasure trove of riches from many centuries of deep history. "The great Talmudic scholar, Musa ibn Maimun, known to the western world as Moses Maimonides, was one of [the] members" of this synagogue. "The twelfth-century Hebrew poet, Judah Halevy is known to have prayed there as well" ("Slave" 165).

[71] For a discussion of the Mamluk dynasty of slave-rulers in Egypt and Syria from the thirteenth to the sixteenth centuries, see *Race*, 144–161. For a study of pan-Mediterranean slavery sourced from the Black Sea regions, see Barker.

he returns, with Leif affectionately calling him "foster-father" (Magnusson and Palsson 55, 57). Ties of fictive kinship, indeed.

Students are afforded several views, in our global texts, of the multifariousness of medieval enslavement: They glimpse a German domestic in a Nordic household who is treated like a member of the family (Magnusson and Palsson 57); see slave-soldiers accompany an Abbasid embassy to the Volga; and find an Indian business agent of a Jewish merchant in the Indian Ocean trade accompanying valuable cargos.

In Kamaluddin Abdul-Razzaq Samarqandi's *Mission to Calicut and Vijayanagar* (henceforth *Vijayanagar*) the vizier of the Indian empire of Vijayanagar, who leads the army to war against the kingdom of Gulbarga, is a eunuch, like Zheng He, the Yunnanese Muslim admiral who helms the convoy of Ming China's "treasure ships" that reach African shores (*Vijayanagar* 315). In Abu Zayd al-Sirafi's *Accounts of China and India*, the eunuch court officials of Tang China are also seen to have immense status and authority. Early global literature opens a multifaceted window into the lives of the (once-)unfree.

Through skillful sleuthing and some dexterous reasoning, Ghosh arrives at a plausible name for the anonymous Indian – Bomma – even hazarding some colorful details about "Ben Yiju's toddy-loving slave, Bomma, the Bhuta-worshiping fisherman from Tulunad" ("Slave" 214). When Ghosh comes to some of his necessarily speculative conclusions, because the archive can disclose only so much, he is as responsible as his love of his subject and fidelity to scholarship enable him to be.

"Slave" is thus an example – like Suzanne Bartlet's and Patricia Skinner's *Licoricia of Winchester*, which attempts to piece together the details of a Jewish woman's life from the often-hostile records of medieval England – of how to respond to the silences of the archive: how to responsibly, ethically, attempt what Saidiya Hartman calls forms of "critical fabulation" when you are confronted with a void, and trying to "imagine what might have happened or might have been said or might have been done," in moments when you need extrapolative scholarship, so as to reach some half-way satisfactory answers (Hartman 12).

A critical imagination no doubt comes more readily to Ghosh than most, a scholar who is primarily a novelist. Indeed, Ghosh's skills as a storyteller are everywhere on display: *Antique Land feels* like a novel, students say, even when its title emphatically announces that it is not. The book's structure – episodes of ethnographic narrative from Ghosh's anthropological fieldwork at two Egyptian villages, Lataifa and Nashawy, intercut by re-creation of events from the twelfth-century world of Abraham and Bomma – saturates the distant past with vivacious immediacy, even as it historicizes the present.

To do this, Ghosh carefully fashions hinges to interface past and present. A prospective marriage between a formerly-impoverished *fellah*, Eid, who made enough money working construction in Saudi Arabia to afford a marriage-payment for an "educated wife" from a "well-off" family is promptly followed by an episode about another trans-class marriage – the union of the well-to-do Abraham to an Indian slave-woman, Ashu, whom Abraham manumits (as witnessed in a deed of 17 February 1132) because, Ghosh reasons, he likely married her (*AL* 226, 215, 227).

The departure of two young friends, Nabeel and Ismail, for extended work in Iraq, becomes an occasion to ask why Abraham's own departure makes him stay away from Egypt for nearly two decades, when other India merchants journeyed back and forth: Ghosh reasons that it is blood-feud which causes Abraham's long sojourn in Malabar, and that historical blood-feud then links to a modern blood-feud, when a dead Egyptian's kinsmen do not receive blood-money compensation (*AL* 161–162, 136).

Antique Land's hinges eloquently function to suggest that the present and past are intricately interwoven, with Egypt and India, too, being interlinked.[72] Time and distance collapse; resemblances between past and present, countries and coasts, magically appear.

A twentieth-century Egyptian village is lodged in medieval time: To peasants, life is still a cycle of work in the fields, punctuated by the occasional *mowlid* or religious festival, ruled by the seasons, faith, and folkways. Modernity exists in urban metropoles, and love – whether marriage to one you love, or frequenting sex workers – is for city folk; *fellaheen* marry someone their family chooses, and birth extra field hands for labor, like always (*AL* 215–220). Ghosh's Egyptian informants even talk like premodern peasants: One asks if it's possible to reach India, riding on a donkey (*AL* 172–173).

Egypt and India, too, are not so different. Ghosh assures his informants that villagers in India live in mud houses and also use oxen for farming. The mischievous humor he occasionally unleashes at the expense of the villagers fails, of course, to strictly follow the participant-observer's playbook for undertaking fieldwork when embedding in a community, but arises when Ghosh is frustrated at being repeatedly made by his informants into *the other*, who must represent all of India.

Race-as-religion rears its head incessantly: Ghosh's village informants, who are Sunni Muslims (but believe in saints and ghosts), repeatedly tell him that as an Indian, and (nominally) Hindu, he must stop *sati* and bride-burning, and

---

[72] Even language performs as a hinge: Ghosh finds the twelfth-century Judeo-Arabic of the Genizah documents oddly similar to the dialectal village Arabic of Lataifa and Nashawy (*AL* 104–105).

indeed, all cremations in India, as well as "cow-worship" in his infidel country; he must get circumcised, and marry a nice Muslim girl – be more like them, in other words. Assumed as an expert on India-manufactured water-pumps, because he's Indian, the anthropologist has an up-front-and-personal view – sometimes hilariously, sometimes annoyingly – of how racial-religious essentialism works in intercultural encounters.

The way that religion, like race, functions to deliver absolute and fundamental differences among humans, in the past and today, is forcibly brought home in a terrifying memory from Ghosh's childhood in Dhaka after Partition, when religious-communal riots between Muslims and Hindus are rife in India and Pakistan, and Ghosh's family's residential compound must serve as a sanctuary for terrified Hindus pursued by a Muslim mob[73] (*AL* 204–210).

In these modern-day encounters, the opacity of the other, and the failure to understand the other, are repeated themes. But an incandescent moment cuts a path through it all, when one villager succeeds in seeing from the viewpoint of the other. Nabeel, one of the two who later leave for work in Iraq, is looking around Ghosh's kitchen while Ghosh is making tea, and suddenly exclaims to the anthropologist: "It must make you think of all the people you left at home . . . when you put that kettle on the stove with just enough water for yourself" (*AL* 151–152).

This extraordinary instant, when the gaze of the anthropologist upon his subjects is suddenly turned back by a subject onto the anthropologist himself, witnesses an empathy that startlingly, momentarily, sends a bridge across chasmic differences. Ghosh's characterization of the sensitive, intelligent Nabeel is inspired: An unlettered *fellah* from an impoverished, nondescript hamlet suddenly becomes unforgettable.

Given that characterization of Nabeel, when he and Ismail depart for oil-rich Iraq as migrant workers – becoming foreign labor under contemporary globalization, so as to earn money for their families back home in their hamlet – we can ask students if the characterization helps us to grasp, in the two friends' deeply humanized faces and personalities, what it's like for migrant workers in the US and elsewhere today.

---

[73] While the violence and terror in the episode reads like a description of race riots, it is Dipesh Chakrabarty, not Ghosh, who calls "religious communalism" in South Asia by the name of *race*: "I have often thought about how we refuse to see the 'racisms' we, as Indians, practise towards one another. For instance, accounts of 'communalist' behaviour are often difficult to distinguish from what in the context of a Western country we will easily decry as 'racist behaviour'" . . . . [W]hy do we use the term racism as if it were something that only the whites did to the non-whites?" (Ghosh and Chakrabarty 154). As Ghosh demurs, Chakrabarty insists, "there are homologies between racism and communalism" (165).

Can we think and empathize – that is, follow Nabeel's lead – to see, and understand something of the poverty that migrant workers come from, and the people they must leave behind, when they labor in a foreign land? I ask: Does this help us to think more sympathetically about undocumented workers today?

In the end, Ghosh's juxtaposition of contemporary globalization – with its narrative of "development" that has youths from "underdeveloped" countries working overseas in richer or more "developed" countries – over and against the twelfth-century globalism of the Indian Ocean trade, finds more tolerance and acceptance in the past than today, across race, class, and religion.

After all, Bomma, the Indian slave from the Malabar coast, who is neither Muslim nor Jewish nor Arab, is trusted, depended on, manumitted, and eventually earns the title of Shaikh for himself (*AL* 266). Ashu, Abraham's wife from the Nair clan of Kerala, who was also a slave, and, Ghosh deduces, possibly even a sex worker in her earlier life, is also manumitted, and bears the Jewish merchant two children (*AL* 226–230) who eventually return to Egypt with their father (*AL* 302).

Compared with the globalism of the twelfth century, which seems to offer social mobility even to the most subaltern of subjects, contemporary globalization, *Antique Land* seems to say, highlights the inequality of nations, and the plight of migrant workers laboring in wealthy lands. While the communities of the Indian Ocean are known to have traded peaceably for centuries before the arrival of the Portuguese, and European imperialism, present-day globalization is shown to be fraught with uneven development that squeezes work opportunities and socioeconomic mobility at home, and witnesses exploitative labor practices, danger, and violence abroad.

In the end, as Ghosh triumphantly retrieves Bomma from anonymity, bearing a name, an ethnicity, a social background, an occupation, and even a personality of sorts, the sensitive Nabeel vanishes in Saddam Hussein's Iraq, when he delays his departure for too long, either because "he always needed to think a long time about everything," or because he was hoping to earn just a little more for his family (*AL* 353). Ghosh tries to imagine how Nabeel might have died, replaying in his mind scenes of frenzied riots in Iraq, in which unarmed, hapless Egyptian workers are attacked by resentful, angry Iraqis (*AL* 350–353).

Just as Ghosh manages to pull one subaltern subject from the anonymity of history, therefore, he loses a friend who understood what it meant to be alone in a foreign land: Nabeel, who would, in time, become nameless and forgotten, yet another subaltern subject in the detritus of the past, lost to history.

As touchstones for two kinds of globalism, one in the past, and the other in the present, Bomma and Nabeel present much for students to think about.

Teaching Kamaluddin Abdul-Razzaq Samarqandi's *Mission to Calicut and Vijayanagar*

Half a millennium after the ruler of the Abbasid Empire, the Caliph al-Muqtadir, sent an embassy responding to a request by a Muslim king in a distant land, another Muslim ruler – the Khagan Shahrukh Mirza, youngest son of Timur Lenkh ("Tamerlane," to the West), and ruler of the Turko-Mongol Timurid Empire of Central Asia – also sent an embassy responding to a request by a Muslim king in a distant land: this time to Calicut, on the Malabar coast of the Indian subcontinent.

Diplomacy with religious overtones, we see, is a robust imperative that drives the arterial pathways of early globalism over many centuries, whether across great landmasses or across turbulent seas. Shahrukh's emissary, Kamaluddin Abdul-Razzaq Samarqandi, gifts us an account of his journey – from Herat in 1442 to the Kingdom of Calicut, and thereafter to the Empire of Vijayanagar – that is as lively as Ibn Fadlan's, but even more colorful, because his narratorial personality is more opinionated and voluble, and his style more erudite and self-referential, breaking into verse whenever the author wants to explore a subject with emphasis and intensity.[74]

Moreover, students attuned to race quickly notice that *Vijayanagar* contains racial epithets early in the narrative. India is "that dark region," and essentialist references to "the glibness of Iraqis" and "the mysteriousness of Indians" begin the inventory of how the narrator characterizes foreign ethnoraces (299, 300). The South Asians Abdul-Razzaq meets, when he arrives in Calicut, are reduced to "Naked blacks with loin cloths tied from their navels to their knees," with their king "as naked as other Hindus" (305).

In this hot, humid land, the envoy makes no concession to reasonableness in dressing for the climate: Meeting with "a *group* of Muslims" but "a *horde* of infidels," he approvingly notes that "the Muslims wear fine clothing in the Arab fashion" whereas "king and beggar" in Calicut (very sensibly, we might think) only wear dhotis, and are thus "naked" savages (305, emphasis added). The racialization of foreign others ("I saw a people the likes of whom I had never imagined") makes Abdul-Razzaq burst into verse:

> A strange nation, neither men nor demons, at
> meeting whom the mind would go mad.
> Had I seen the likes of them in a dream, my
> heart would have been upset for years.
> I am comfortable with those whose faces are
> like the moon, not with *every ill-proportioned*
> *black thing* (304–305, emphasis added)

---

[74] Page numbers refer to Thackston.

Difficult to acknowledge as human because of skin color and dress, the inhabitants of this "strange nation" are reduced to "every ill-proportioned black thing" (305). If we saw the practice of Orientalism without an Orient, in Ibn Fadlan, in Abdul-Razzaq we see Orientalism practiced in a double-Orient: Here, a man from a "nearer" east is gazing upon those in a "farther" east – Central Asia gazing upon South Asia – and denigrating South Asians. Do we call this Orientalism too? Abdul-Razzaq's racialization of others doesn't even end at "that abode of infidels," with "their unacceptable worship" but extends to those nearer home as well: Hormuzis, he says, have "mischief" "ingrained in their nature" which makes them "seize opportunities for vileness" (315, 307).

Vijayanagar is thus an excellent text with which to continue discussions of critical concepts like Orientalism and explore *why* and *when* race-making occurs. In premodern global texts, the overlap between *race* and *religion* happens with some regularity, not only in texts of encounter authored by Muslims but also those authored by Christians and others. Because Abdul-Razzaq is in India, his racializing discourse often hinges on *skin color* – epidermal race.

If you teach the *Arabian Nights*, where some stories feature treacherous, dangerous black slaves, and black low-class villains who seduce women of incomprehensible sexual appetites, *Vijayanagar*'s juxtaposition of "those with faces like the moon" – a praise-formula common in the *Nights* – against "every ill-proportioned black thing" furnishes a nexus of references with a long shadow.

But it is necessary to point out that racialization in *Vijayanagar* has *two* axes: issuing descriptions that castigate, and descriptions that *exoticize* difference.

Once the Timurid envoy reaches the capital city of Vijayanagar (bearing the same name as the empire – see Fig. 3), that global city's otherness and difference effloresces as *sensuality, spectacle,* and *exorbitance*: Exotic bazaars teem with aromatic flowers in profusion; jewelers display pearls, diamonds, rubies, and emeralds for sale; an elephantorium supplies a thousand domesticated, wondrous beasts for the *Mahanavami* festival; brothels feature finely-dressed, exquisitely-bejeweled courtesans of great beauty; and, as exotically, a police force (to ensure the safety of brothel-clients' possessions) is paid wages from taxation on the earnings of the lovely sex workers (308–310, 313).

Indeed, Abdul-Razzaq is so dazzled by the city of Vijayanagar that we no longer hear complaints that Indians are ill-proportioned black things; instead, the inhabitants of Vijayanagar, a city with seven concentric walls, "have no equal in the world" (307).[75]

---

[75] I sometimes ask students to draw a city plan of Vijayanagar, as a way to visualize the different districts of this Indian global city, and the economic and social relations of the city's spaces.

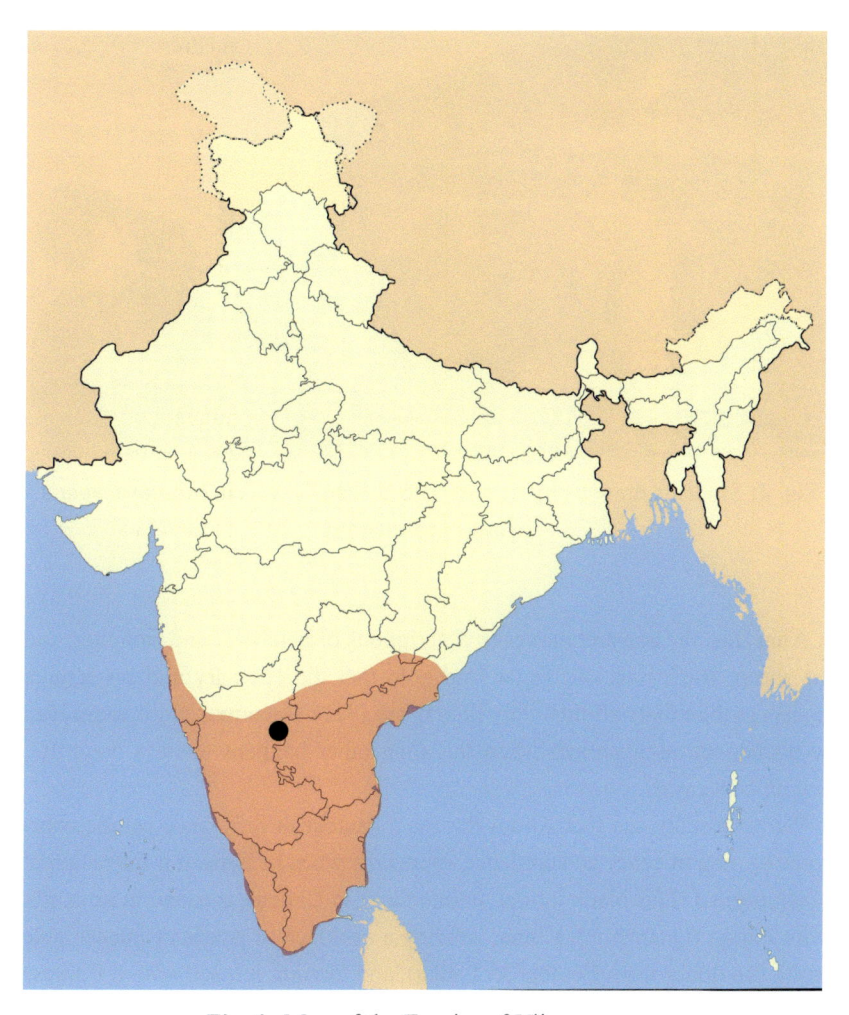

Fig. 3: Map of the Empire of Vijayanagar

The emperor – Deva Raya II – is admittedly "dark of complexion," but has a "pleasant" face (307). Seated in architectonic splendor, he wears "a tunic of Zaytuni silk and a necklace of lustrous pearls, the worth of which the jeweler of the mind could scarcely appraise" (310). Rather than dwell on the emperor's skin color, the narrator shifts to the emperor's thoughtfulness: Deva Raya gives Abdul-Razzaq, who was "perspiring profusely from the heat and all the clothes I was wearing" (because Abdul-Razzaq is not a "naked" local in a "loin-cloth"), the emperor's own Chinese fan to use.

From left to right, in Fig. 4, are: Maddox Michener, Delacey Bouchard, Lauryn Midgett, and James Sam.

Fig. 4: Students draw a city plan of Vijayanagar, to visualize Vijayanagar's districts and quarters

After this, the account moves to descriptions of betel-leaf and camphor, and the sheep, fowl, rice, oil, sugar, and gold that the emissary and his retinue receive as their daily allotment for their needs (311). Race-making, it seems, can be abandoned as a project when the alien other happens to be a bountiful, magnificent royal.

We bemusedly see that Abdul-Razzaq's hauteur at difference can be overcome by magnificence and opulence, especially when he himself is the recipient of abundance. *This* black infidel, unlike those in Calicut, is robed in satin silk from Zaitun (Quanzhou), China, wearing a necklace of pearls of incalculable worth (no doubt from Ceylon/Sri Lanka), and fanning himself with a Chinese fan: a perfect picture of early globalism crystallized upon one person.

Other moments exist when Abdul-Razzaq's abhorrence is similarly overridden, such as when he witnesses sculptural artistry and aesthetic beauty in South Asia. At Mangalore, he finds an "idol temple" with "a statue in the likeness of a human being, full stature, made of gold. It had two red rubies for eyes, so cunningly made that you would say it could see" (306). Rather than denounce this idol, the envoy is moved to exclaim: "What craft and artisanship!" (306).

In Pednur, the Timurid envoy finds "buildings and beauties" that were like "the houris and palaces of paradise," innumerable flowers, cypresses that make him rhapsodize, verdant plane trees that draw poeticisms from him, and temple carvings of dark blue stone of exquisite intricacy and "extreme delicacy," with "so many designs," that he must break into verse *twice* (306–307).

It's therefore crucial to discuss with students how *art* in the widest sense of the word, encompassing Quranic recitation in Ibn Fadlan, and temple architecture (see, e.g., Fig. 5) and artisanry in Abdul-Razzaq, as well as *natural beauty* – flowers, cypresses, and plane trees in India, the aurora borealis of the Eurasian steppe – can form bridges across difference in narratives of encounter where otherwise denigration and othering might occur.[76] Students can be asked to find modern occasions when art and natural beauty also forge bridges across difference, resulting in the appreciation of otherness.

Abdul-Razzaq's admiration of beauty, of course, includes a lively admiration of *female* beauty. His gaze lingers on the courtesans of Vijayanagar, who are "quite young and extremely beautiful" who are ready for "pleasure, revelry and enjoyment" and "willing to dally with anyone" (310). The emissary reports a good deal about Vijayanagar's brothels, from the fact that the lovely courtesans have serving women, to the safekeeping of "customers' belongings" which, if lost while the customers are indulging themselves, are made good and compensated. The "beauty, blandishments, and attraction" of these courtesans may be sampled at "many similar brothels" of the city, apparently (311).

Fig. 5: A Vijayanagar temple with carvings, sculpture, and reliefs

---

[76] Abdul-Razzaq's rhapsodizing over betel-leaf (he devotes a long poem to the chewable that is ubiquitous in South Asia and Indic Southeast Asia) also suggests that select alien foodstuffs, especially spices and delectables, can also form bridges across difference (311).

The Timurid is equally cow-eyed at female artistes – singers and dancers, but especially the dancers – at the *Mahanavami* festival, who have "cheeks like the moon . . . with beautiful garments and enchanting countenances like fresh roses" and who "dance in an astonishingly enchanting manner" (313), and offers up one of his more ecstatic verses:

> A hundred female singers, a crowd filled with
> moons and Jupiters.
> When they removed the veil from the sun,
> with one wink they destroyed the world.
> With countenances shining like the sun, they
> scorched people's souls with their fire.
> When the veil was dropped from their faces,
> the moon went veiled into a pit.
> When they danced, their statures were musky
> locks sweeping the ground.
> When they struck the ground with their
> dancing feet, they kicked Venus from
> competition.
> The audience were all astonished by their
> motion and movement (313–314)

Apparently, Abdul-Razzaq never saw beautifully performed Indian classical dance (*bharatanatyam*? See Fig. 6) before, so the ecstatic clamor here owes both to his effusive style and his discovery of yet another bridge across difference and otherness. Do ask students how they feel about these kinds of gendered, sexualized, and ambiguous bridges across difference.

There is much in *Vijayanagar* to discuss – from disquisitions on India's elephants and architecture, to what a global city in South Asia looks like, to the author's opulent style and many poems, some of which are exquisite, while others are hyperbolically hilarious – but Abdul-Razzaq's account is particularly useful for its eloquent descriptions of the experience of sea journeys for those who are not seasoned mariners.

Where Ibn Fadlan is expressive about extreme cold, and the grindingly slow progress of camel caravans across a landmass, Abdul-Razzaq is voluble on the terrors of sea journeys, the turbulence of the Indian ocean, monsoons dictating when and in which direction it is possible to travel; seasons of rampant piracy; and even "the smell of the ship" in one's nostrils (300).

This terrified landlubber suffers from motion sickness, febrile fever, hallucinatory dreams, infections, and just about every ailment imaginable on his maritime journeys, to all of which he gives prolix testimony, and about which he issues profusely romantic lyric poetry. Likening himself to Moses cast on the

Fig. 6: An Indian classical dancer of *Bharatanatyam* striking a pose

waters, and to Al-Khizr, the Timurid ambassador quaveringly tells us he "gave up all hope of life" more than once (302).

Indeed, we are so volubly treated to the "terrors of a sea voyage," and how it feels to be stranded when the monsoons do not cooperate, that students who had wondered what crossing an ocean was like for premodern peoples, and had wanted more from the *Vinland Sagas*' terse, spare accounts of voyaging, have their curiosity more than amply satisfied in this text.

To satisfy curiosity about what it might be like to view oceans *not* as crucibles of ordeal and dread, but as roadways that join civilizations and cultures, I try to include in syllabi a unit on maritime worlds and societies, with at least one text ostensibly produced by mariners themselves. We turn next to sailors' stories, merchants' accounts of far-flung maritime trade, and the worlds of island Southeast Asia.

7 Oceans of Stories, and Island Worlds: Teaching Buzurg ibn Shahriyar's *The Book of the Wonders of India: Mainland, Sea and Islands*, and Abu Zayd al-Sirafi's *Accounts of China and India*, with *the Malay Annals*

Two eye-opening accounts of what premodern peoples who were accustomed to sea travel thought and felt, as they traversed the watery worlds of maritime Asia, are a tenth-century compilation of mariners' tales attributed to a sea captain from Ramhormuz in Khuzistan, Buzurg ibn Shahriyar, and a ninth-and-tenth-century compilation of merchants' news and anecdotal reports attributed to Abu Zayd al-Sirafi in the Persian Gulf.

The more colorful of the two, *The Book of the Wonders of India: Mainland, Sea and Islands*, edited and translated by G. S. P. Freeman-Grenville, can be taught as a lively companion-text to the *Arabian Nights*, whose tall tales of bizarre marvels, and wild stories of fictional maritime adventurers in ocean worlds, are easily rivaled, even trumped, by the sea captain's account of sailors' tales offered as lived experiences, however bizarre, sometimes with the names of witnesses and participants attached to them.[77]

Abu Zayd's merchant-focused compilation, *Accounts of China and India*, translated by Tim Mackintosh-Smith – Book One of which is not authored by Abu Zayd, but attributed to Sulayman al-Tajir ("Sulayman the Merchant") – has been considered a "mother lode" of historical information on Asia before the much later accounts of Polo-Rustichello and Ibn Battuta (5, 13).[78] Often consulted for its report on mercantilism in Tang China, and the rebellion of Huang Chao, which resulted in the 878–879 massacre of 120,000 foreign merchants – Arabs, Persians, and Jews[79] – in the port-city of Guangdong, Abu Zayd's compilation is a cherished data trove.

These accounts contain vivid descriptions of China and India before the eleventh century and can be fruitfully taught with later texts such as Polo-Rustichello's on thirteenth-century China, or Abdul-Razzaq's on fifteenth-century India (or Al-Biruni's on Indic philosophy and religious cultural history), among others.

As importantly, these texts feature details about island Southeast Asia, archipelagos famed for their spices, rare woods, aromatics, and resins – and referred to in European texts like *Mandeville's Travels* as the "5,000 isles of India," because of the influence of Indic religion and culture in the islands before Islam's arrival – as well as mainland Southeast Asia. Book One of Abu Zayd's compilation even offers a ninth-century glimpse of Korea.

The three texts in this section thus together map a mosaic of maritime worlds and arterial pathways that encompass oceanic movements of news, objects, peoples, ideas, and religion across watery geographic distances – worlds that are linked by seas and ships, and where people and polities live lives, and sustain economies, that are dependent on oceans and seas.

Teaching Buzurg ibn Shahriyar's *Book of the Wonders of India: Mainland, Sea and Islands*

Accounts of caravan journeys and sea voyages address a question sometimes asked by students: Where do the luxury goods, silks, spices, gems, pearls,

---

[77] Recent scholarship suggests this text is likely not authored by Ibn Shahriyar, but I retain the tradition of the sea captain's narratorial persona here. Page numbers refer to Freeman-Grenville.

[78] Page numbers refer to Mackintosh-Smith.

[79] Abu Zayd lists the foreign mercantile communities by religion: "Muslims, Jews, Christians, and Zoroastrians" (69). The historian Al-Masudi has the massacred at 200,000 (140 n.84).

perfumes, porcelain, and rare delicacies that appear in medieval European romances, and the *Arabian Nights,* come from, and what can we know about them?

Buzurg ibn Shahriyar's collection of stories, haphazardly told in no particular order or with any semblance of organization, shows us that the sailors who manned ocean-going vessels, and the merchants who accompanied cargoes from the Persian Gulf, Arabia, and Africa across the Indian Ocean and Bay of Bengal to the China sea and back, embarked on their long-distance journeys because of the gigantic profits and immense wealth to be gained from precious cargoes of luxury goods too heavy and massive to be transported by land caravans alone.[80]

These stories, narrated through what seems like free association, thus expressively convey the historical basis of the material luxuries depicted in recreational literature, serving as an accounting of sorts for how the extravagant tissue of material culture that imparts an aura of elite life in recreational literature is attained for the societies producing that literature.

The chatty sea captain from Ramhormuz shows us the terrible travails at sea that is the price of such commercial conveyance: perils from storms, gales, and giant waves that beggar description; sudden risk of enslavement, impoverishment, and death; bizarre monsters and creatures that rival any in the *Arabian Nights*. We see that the standard practice to save a ship in a tempest is to lighten it by tossing out its cargo: a survival strategy that means the loss of a fortune. So, once a fortune has indeed been made, mariners tell us with relief, "From that day on we have given up sailing" (45).

Despite the perils of using oceans as roads, however, some intrepid sailors are renowned for repeated trans-world voyaging. A certain Captain Abhara, who "sailed the sea in all directions," makes the months-long route from the Gulf to China and back *seven times* (50): "No one had done it without an accident," we are told, "If a man reached China without dying on the way, it was already a miracle. Returning safe and sound was unheard of. I had never heard tell of anyone [else] … who had made … two voyages there and back without mishap" (50).

We also learn, astonishingly, that cargo lost at sea might turn up again, to reward the virtuous, the pious, or the lucky – a story-trope that makes these mariners' tales greatly resemble the *Arabian Nights* (e.g., 81–82, 84–86).

---

[80] The profit from a ship's cargo could be ten times the cost of the capital for the merchandise (28), and a dhow plying the route between the Gulf and China could carry many times the weight of an overland caravan. Till the eighth-century advent of ocean-going vessels, the great demand in the Near East for Chinese porcelain and ceramics could scarcely be met by overland routes alone (for the sea routes, see Fig. 7). One shipwreck, off Belitung Island in Indonesia, shows that an ocean-going dhow could carry 70,000 ceramic items on a single journey (Heng,"An Ordinary Ship").

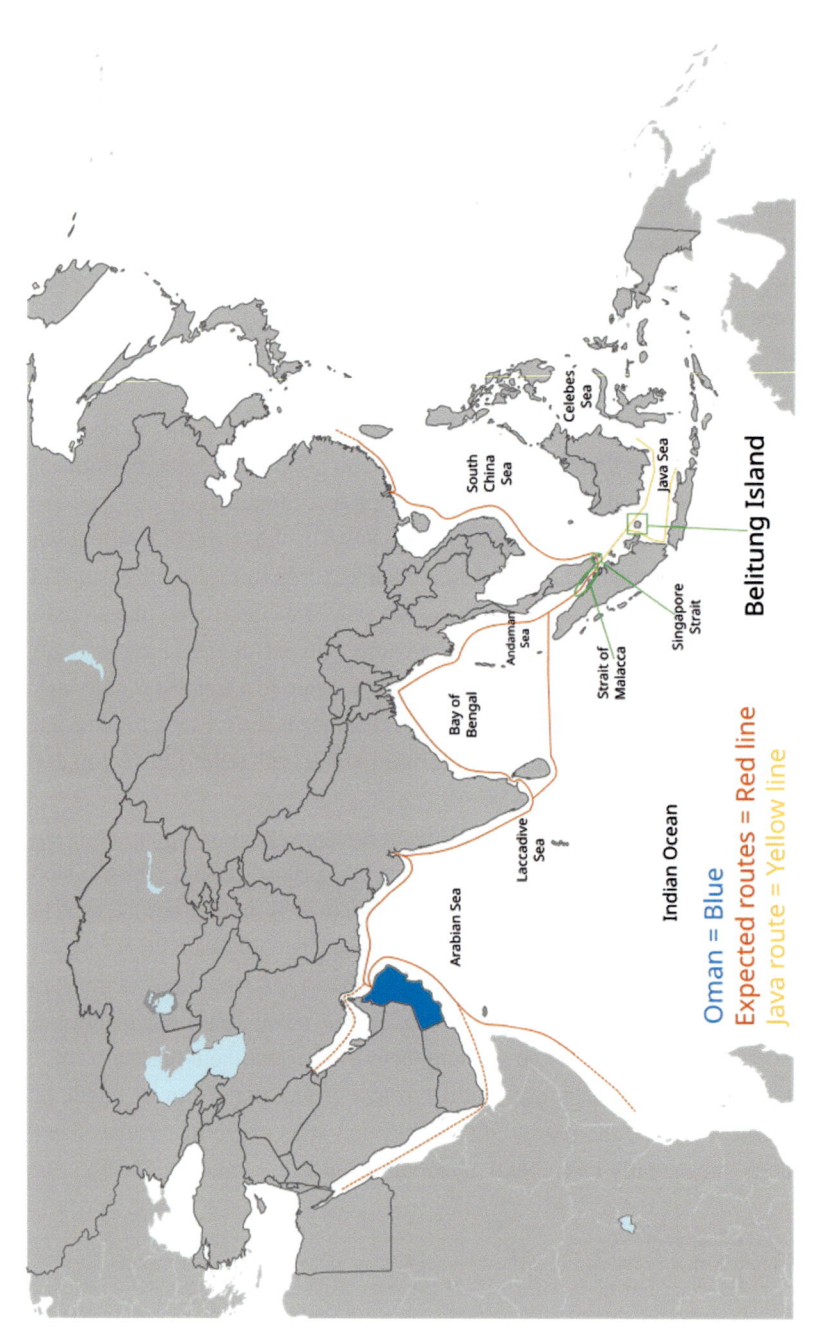

Fig. 7: The transglobal sea routes of the China trade

Oman = Blue

Expected routes = Red line

Java route = Yellow line

Belitung Island

Indian Ocean

South China Sea

Celebes Sea

Java Sea

Andaman Sea

Bay of Bengal

Strait of Malacca

Singapore Strait

Laccadive Sea

Arabian Sea

The ocean as a crucible of opportunity means we get to see how the enslaved persons we encounter in global literature might have become enslaved in the first place. Ismailawayh, a captain to whom several tales are attributed, relates a vignette in which he and others are blown off course to East Africa, to "Sofala on the Zanj coast" (31).[81] Initially terrified of the Africans – whom they deem "cannibal negroes" – the mariners are warmly and civilly welcomed. The African king graciously allows them to trade "without any hindrances or customs duties," treating them with courtesy and generosity (31).[82]

Despite (or because of?) the king's kindness, however, Captain Ismailawayh muses that "In the market in Oman this young king would certainly fetch thirty dinars, and his seven companions sixty each" (31). Like Thorfinn Karlsefni, Ismailawayh's calculations quickly turn to international markets – slave markets, this time. The mariners kidnap, enslave, and sell the African king and his people. Altogether, the text relates, Ismailawayh and his sailors sell about 200 slaves in Oman.

The story of this nameless African king eventually becomes a tale of his escape, conversion to Islam, and adventures that lead him home to resume his kingship, so that his tale becomes a parable of triumphal virtuous behavior, a parable again reminiscent of the *Arabian Nights*. The seamen meet him a second time, when they are again blown off course, and, terrified once more, become remorseful of their abhorrent behavior when he lessons them. The African king again behaves exemplarily, but expresses profound contempt for them.

So, this story turns on failed racist stereotypes about Black Africans, ethical versus execrable conduct, and divine providence. Students will also remark how medieval slavery depends on ad hoc opportunism. Initially expecting to be preyed on by the *Zanj* whom they malign, the mariners quickly become predators instead – economic cannibals preying on a virtuous king and his good people. Soberingly, East Africans as potential slaves is a repeating trope: In another story, one Ibn Lakis says the people of the Waq-waq islands attacked Qanbalu, because "they wanted to obtain Zanj, for they were strong and easily endured slavery" (103).[83]

Exercised whenever conditions allow it, opportunistic slavery – including enslaving children – appears fairly ubiquitous, and the buying and selling of

---

[81] *Zanj*, in Arabic texts, tends to refer to Black Africans living south of Ethiopia in East Africa, including the Swahili coast.

[82] By contrast, custom duties imposed by the Sultan of Oman amounted to 10 percent of a cargo's value (62), while port taxes imposed by the Emperor of China in Guangzhou amounted to 30 percent of a cargo's value (45).

[83] Waq-waq, designating an island or islands in Arabic texts, has not been identified with any known place, and appears fictitious, though "They say there are about 30,000 of these islands, and merchants say about 12,000 of them are inhabited" (95).

humans, slaveholding, and slave revolts are narrated with some predictability (e.g., 7, 19–20, 18–21, 31–33). It seems that whenever a ship arrives, locals hide, for good reason, since sailors and merchants appear to treat all humans as acquirable commodities whenever they can.

And not merely humans: Monkeys are enslaved with some frequency and perform menial domestic tasks and hard labor and are also used for sex. One sex slave is a mermaid: Chained up for eighteen years after she fails to escape, she is forced to bear six children by her master, and, when finally released by her children on the death of their father, she flees for her life (19–21).

A usage mentality thus pervades many stories: Enslave people when you can, including children; eat and use animals any way you can, including using animals for sex; and take advantage of others before they take advantage of you. Like the *Arabian Nights*, stories revolve around jealousy, competitiveness, and greed; with a few turning on exemplarily virtuous people. All manner of creatures appear – whales, turtles, fish, birds, snakes, crocodiles, ants – in behavior and sizes natural and monstrous.

Like the *Nights*, these mariners' tales also detail transgressive sexual practices, but the stories here are even more ribald. While the *Nights* depict oversexed women, sibling incest, and hint at covert homoerotic behavior, these seamen's tales feature *explicit* homoerotic overtures, the rape of women and sheep, bestiality with monkeys and fish that births hybrid creatures, a mermaid sex slave, and even sex with a statue, detected through the presence of the culprit's semen on the statue (46, 82–83, 107, 40–41, 20, 19–21, 83).

Women, in these sailors' tales and the *Nights*, are of course ready and eager for sex. While European romances depict castles of maidens that possibly derive from rumors about harems in the East, these seamen's tales tell of "an island" where only women reside, so that sailors who are blown ashore are greeted by "a thousand women, or more" for each man, who "compelled them to become the tools of their pleasure" (16–17). The price of all this pleasure is that "The men died of exhaustion one after the other." And, of course, the women all "want to dominate" men (17).

In the stories' treatment of otherness, we hear about "cannibal Zanj" in Africa (104) and cannibal natives of the East Indies, but tellingly, the sole witnessed incident of (almost-)cannibalism involves mariners and merchants themselves. During a storm where a ship carrying cargo of "incalculable value" is lost, thirty-three men who get into a lifeboat are storm-tossed for five days, experiencing such hunger and thirst that they decide to eat "a very fat boy" whose father, like the captain, had gone down with the ship (97, 98). Fortuitously, this intended cannibalism is aborted when the boat washes ashore, and villagers arrive to succor everyone (98).

Cannibalism, often attributed as a marker to distinguish uncivilized peoples from civilized peoples, is a slippery identifier in these stories. These sailors' tales can end up undercutting their trajectory of othering by pointing to execrable behavior exhibited by the sailors themselves rather than by the othered. See what students think about this.

Finally, our inescapable impression is that mariners go to sea because of cargoes. Pilgrims, envoys, and others may be passengers, but the oceanic waterways of the world beckon because of their promise of profit and wealth.

Teaching Abu Zayd al-Sirafi's *Accounts of China and India*

Abu Zayd al-Hasan al-Sirafi's *Accounts of China and India* is even more concerned with how profit accrues. Unlike the sea captain's salty stories, Abu Zayd declares that *his* collection eschews mariners' tales (133).[84] Instead, the compilation delivers helpful descriptions of taxes, ports, merchandise, laws, and practical information like where freshwater can be found.

Nonetheless, encounters with foreign others still reliably produce cannibals. In the Andaman Islands, cannibals "eat anyone who passed by them" and eat them alive (27). Andaman cannibals "are black and have frizzy hair, with hideous faces and eyes" (27). Between Ceylon/Sri Lanka ("Sarandib") and Kedah ("Kalah") in coastal Malaya, there resides "a tribe of negroes who are naked and who, if they find anyone from outside their land, hang him upside down, cut him into pieces, and devour him raw" (35).[85]

These cannibal societies are doubly uncivilized, since they not only eat people, but one eats people *alive*, and the other eats people *raw*. Further east, in Sumatra ("al-Ramani") where gold, sapan wood, and rattan are found (and where the thriving empire of Srivijaya dominated the region for six centuries), "a tribe who eat people" also exists (25, 27).

But cannibals aren't just black and brown islanders in the Indian Ocean/Bay of Bengal/Andaman Sea/Straits of Malacca. Even China's inhabitants – praised as "fine-looking ... with clear, pale complexions," and lauded as the world's best craftsmen, engravers, and manufacturers ("no one from any other nation has the edge on them"), in a land extolled for law and order, sophisticated

---

[84] See the translator's comments on *akhbar*, accounts of credited historicity supported by chains of witnesses, the relationship between Abu Zayd and al-Masudi (the "Herodotus of the Arabs"), and the use of the compilation by Ibn Khurradadhbih, Ibn al-Faqih, Ibn Rustah, al-Idrisi, al-Qazwini, and Ibn al-Wardi (9–13).

[85] I refer to the Malay peninsula by its older, pre-Independence name, *Malaya*, rather than *Malaysia*, since *Malaysia* encompasses more territories than just peninsular Malaya (commonly referred to now as *West Malaysia*).

bureaucratic management, and boasting megalopolises of two million people – turn cannibal on occasion (55, 77).

"When one of the rulers under the command of the Great King [i.e., the Tang Emperor] acts unjustly . . . they slay him and eat him . . . . Chinese eat the flesh of all who are killed by the sword" (55, 77, 59). In the aftermath of Huang Chao's rebellion, China's warlords "eat all the defeated . . . people, cannibalism being permissible for them according to their legal code, for they trade in human flesh in their markets" (71). Chinese cannibalism, it seems, is *punitive* cannibalism, inflicted on unjust rulers and the people of defeated leaders.[86]

Between opportunistic slavery, and punitive cannibalism, the maritime Silk Road appears to encompass practices and zones that excel at turning humans into commodities and comestibles, according to sailors' and merchants' reports.

While not all cannibals are dark-skinned, and light-skinned Chinese are also cannibals, racial othering in Abu Zayd's compilation seems to link pale skin with beauty, and black skin with ugliness. The pale-skinned Chinese are "a fine-looking people"; in Takka ("al-Taqa") "women . . . are fair-skinned and . . . the most beautiful . . . in India"; and in Kashmir (? "Al-Kashibin") "people are pale-skinned . . . and are good-looking" (55, 41, 43). But Andaman Islanders, who are black, have "frizzy hair, hideous faces and eyes" (27). The racial discourse in this compilation thus conjoins *two* tropes of othering: skin color and cannibalism.[87]

For merchants, however, even the extreme alterity of cannibalism can be overlooked when socioeconomic conditions favor profit and trade, and Abu Zayd's compilation is full of admiration for Tang China's bureaucracy, laws, and judicial system.

Tang bureaucracy ensures "Chinese act fairly where financial dealings or debts are concerned," with debts being recorded on chirographs bearing finger marks (and seals?) and accreting a paper trail for repayment (51). Nonpayment triggers intensive investigation and draconian state punishment – a substantial monetary fine plus "twenty blows on the back with wooden staves," enough to kill a man (53). If a debtor is genuinely bankrupt, however, a creditor is "paid

---

[86] An adulterer is putatively punished by having his body contorted into a kind of pretzel, then executed by being beaten to death, after which "he is given over to those who will eat him" (73).

[87] Foreigners who don clothing from neck to feet, like the Arabs, are mentioned with greater sympathy than those who are "naked," wearing only "waist cloths": "The Chinese are better-looking than the Indians and more like the Arabs in their dress . . . for they wear long tunics and belts," whereas "Indians wear two waist cloths" (65). Chinese elites are admired for silk so fine, a mole can be glimpsed through five layers of silk, whereas even "the most important Indian dignitaries" wear "nothing but a waist cloth to make themselves decent" (77, 131). Arabic texts on India, from Abu Zayd in the tenth century to Abdul Razzaq in the fifteenth, seem to pounce on the "waist wrappers" or "waist cloths" (dhotis, lunghis) worn by supposedly "naked" Indian men. Discourses of othering pivot on not only what a people eat, but also what they wear.

what they are owed from the treasury" (53). With all this, and the state indemnifying loans, there is no need for "witnesses or oaths" in financial dealings (53).

Clearly, laws like this are of paramount importance to merchants who might otherwise lose money in less-regulated business transactions. China's rules and regulations guarantee that business can be efficaciously transacted, and this report seems to believe the system is fair.

We learn that the state even indemnifies cargoes and merchandise that are lost. Port taxes are high: "three-tenths of the goods are taken in kind, as duty," but the Emperor pays "the very highest prices" for merchandise he wants, "and pays immediately" (45). Rather than complain about the high port taxes, the narrator intones approvingly, "camphor, if the ruler had not bought it, would be only worth half that price on the open market" (45).

Indeed, the system is so laudable, the Emperor even punishes his own officials who mistreat merchants. Rather than have a Khurasani spread news of improper treatment in China, the Emperor admonishes an official who had confiscated the merchant's property – "you exposed me to the risk of losing face," the ruler scolds – and demotes his official for it (99, 101).

That misbegotten official, like others in charge of China's treasury and the Emperor's household and ports, is a *eunuch slave* (75). Students who are following enslaved people in global literature may remember that the vizier of Vijayanagar, who led Vijayanagar's army to war against Muslim Gulbarga, was also a eunuch. We see again that in premodernity, the horrors of castration and slavery can ironically lead to high positions and power:

> eunuch slaves ... function as overseers of taxes and as doorkeepers of the treasury. Some ... are of non-Chinese origin, captured in the borderlands, then castrated; others come from the native Chinese population and are castrated by their fathers, then presented by them to the ruler as a means of gaining favor. All matters to do with the ruler's own household and his treasuries, as well as with foreigners arriving in the city of Khanfu ([Guangzhou] to which the Arab merchants go), all this is the concern of these slaves (75).[88]

In short, the Tang Emperor's exemplary behavior in safeguarding China's reputation has Abu Zayd exclaim with admiration at "the status of the law and the high regard" Chinese have for law and order, despite their ascribed taint of cannibalism (101). The narrator even rhapsodizes over the selection of upright

---

[88] The high status of these "slave officials" is dramatized when the narrator says the populace must evacuate the streets and retire indoors whenever the eunuch officials are out riding in public, so as "to impart a sense of fear and awe and to give the commoners no opportunity of gawping at their masters or daring to address them" (75).

men for judges (103). Law and order, of course, ensures the smooth functioning of the Indian Ocean trade, and China's access to foreign goods, international markets, and large profits.

Its mercantile gaze also means that this compilation is remarkable for the first foreign mention of tea-drinking in China, and the first foreign mention of porcelain made from white kaolin clay into the delicately fine cups and tableware (especially Xing and Ding white wares) for which Tang China was internationally renowned (49, 45).[89]

In sum, Tang China is presented as a shining model of precocious modernity four centuries before Polo-Rustichello present Yuan China as a shining model of precocious modernity. China even has universal literacy ("poor or rich, young or old, all learn how to form letters and to write"), because "every city has a school and a teacher to teach the poor how to write." A welfare system ensures "children of the poor are fed from the public treasury," and any man over eighty pays no tax but "is given a pension from the public treasury" (47, 55).

Universal healthcare sustains the poor: "if a sick person is poor, he is given the cost of his medicine from the public treasury" (55). The Emperor even guards food staples against inflation, releasing stocks from imperial granaries at half price when the cost of grain is too high (49). And Tang China has a pony express – well, a mule express – for sending communications around the country, much like the postal system Polo-Rustichello would describe in Yuan China (107).

Perhaps the most eye-opening example of China's exemplary modernity is its legalization of sex work. The narrator himself is censorious about "women who do not wish to be virtuously married but prefer a life of sexual promiscuity" – as he tendentiously puts it – but the state merely has these women licensed by the chief of police, who records their ancestry, physical appearance, and place of residence (73). Duly registered, a sex worker then practices her profession freely and without hindrance: "she pays her dues annually, and no opprobrium attaches to her" (73).

Of course, Tang China's modernity, like Yuan China's, requires bureaucratic surveillance. A male child must be registered at birth, and men aged eighteen to eighty pay a poll tax, varying by "landed and other property that they own" (55). Girls and women go unmentioned, but the treasury's daily revenue from the poll tax in Guangzhou ("Khanfu") alone totals 50,000 dinars (49). State surveillance also requires two passport documents for travelers, so that identities and provenance can be checked at "guardposts on the road," ensuring no "traveler's

---

[89] For Tang China's international export trade in fine and mass-produced ceramics, see "An Ordinary Ship."

money or goods … go missing" – which is no doubt reassuring to traveling merchants (51). For merchants, of course, state surveillance is a net positive, securing order, and favoring business.

Students thus see that a compilation concerned with mercantile interests has no difficulty discovering bridges across difference. Even if there's cannibalism – an abhorrent marker of difference – Tang China is a shining vision of modernity, admired for its law and order, surveillance system, and state institutions that ensure the smooth functioning of business. Sometimes, bridges across differences are forged in ways and for reasons we do not expect. What do students make of it?

Abu Zayd's compilation also describes what Abdul-Razzaq's account of India omits, but that texts often find striking and iconic about India: cremation on funeral pyres, sati, the caste system, sadhus, and even devadasis – a temple-based system of female sexual service or "prostitution" that bewilders the narrator as much as legalized sex work in China (57, 59, 117, 119). Students can compare how sex workers in Vijayanagar, and in Abu Zayd's India and China, are portrayed.

Both books of the compilation also list the greatest rulers of the world in order of their importance – a weighing of regnal magnitude articulated, ostensibly, by the Chinese themselves (Book One) or voiced by the Tang Emperor (Book Two). Unsurprisingly, the Abbasid Caliph emerges as the paramount ruler on the planet. Book One names "the king of the Arabs" as the "mightiest, the richest in possessions, and the most resplendently fine in appearance," as well as "king of the great religion to which nothing is superior" (39). Next in greatness comes the Emperor of China, then "the Byzantine king," followed by a (Deccan?) king of India dubbed "Balhara" (39).

Book Two has the Tang Emperor himself declare he only considers five kings in the world to be truly great. The Abbasids again take the trophy: "The one with the most extensive realm is he who rules Iraq, for he is at the center of the world, and the other kings are ranged around him" (81). Next, the Tang Emperor considers himself second best, followed by the king of the Turks, the king of India, and the king of Byzantium (79, 81).

What is useful for students to see, in these lists of the greats, is that no king of Latin Europe appears anywhere on the horizon at all. If a key aim of teaching global literature is to decenter Europe, this text is a helpful aid in showing how little the Latin West and its kings figured in the estimation of the great trading empires and networks of the premodern world.

Abu Zayd's is thus a highly useful text to teach. Not only does it trace the routes of the maritime Silk Road, from the Persian Gulf, Arabia, and Africa, all the way to China, but it offers uncommon glimpses of the ports and polities of island Southeast Asia.[90] For an elaboration of those island societies, we turn next to a global text in classical Malay: the *Sejarah Melayu*, or *Malay Annals*.[91]

Teaching the *Malay Annals*

Of the two dozen or so texts in this Element from which to build a syllabus, sadly only a handful are written by a people about themselves. More often, the texts are authored by visitors – diplomats, traders, sailors, missionaries – who render a society from the outside. Too often, these visitors also scarcely refrain from pejorative commentary on the peoples and societies they visit, which are so unlike their own.

By contrast, the *Malay Annals* (translated by C. C. Brown), like the epic of Mali, is narrated by those who are native to the land. It charts how a regional kingdom – the Malacca Sultanate, in peninsular Malaya – arises out of the volatile politics of rival powers in the Malay Archipelago: especially the old empire of Srivijaya (see Fig. 8), based on the island of Sumatra (with its capital at Palembang), and on the decline in the thirteenth century and after, and the upstart, new empire of Majapahit, based on the island of Java, and on the ascendent.[92]

The *Annals* highlights a maritime world, a world of islands and archipelagos. A maritime world is a world in motion, where there is a constant movement of people from place to place, island to island. The stories spread across territories that are today part of Indonesia, Malaysia, and Singapore, linking all these territories back to India and to the great cultural, religious, and linguistic impact of India upon island Southeast Asia, but also back to the Near East, and the Mediterranean, through the global spread of Islam, and the global prestige of the Alexander legend. This is a text that moves through time, and space, in establishing globalism.

Considered "the finest literary work in Malay" (ix), the *Annals*, like the epic of Mali, was set down late, in modern times, from oral traditions. The manuscript on which the English translation is based (Raffles M. S. 18, Library of

---

[90] For an idea of the goods and ships involved in what's been called the maritime silk road, see the Tang Shipwreck at http://www.globalmiddleages.org/project/tang-shipwreck and the exhibit at the Asian Civilisations Museum, Singapore: https://www.nhb.gov.sg/acm/galleries/maritime-trade/tang-shipwreck.

[91] *Malay*, in this Element, is an ethnoracial designation for a Malay person, as well as a linguistic designation, while someone from peninsular Malaya is a *Malayan*. I use the spelling of the *Annals* (e.g., *Malacca*, for today's *Melaka*, and *Temasek*, for today's *Temasik*).

[92] The *Annals* is scarcely interested in Jambi, the supposed capital of the Melayu Kingdom in Sumatra that may have overtaken or replaced a weakened Srivijaya, but focuses on Palembang, the old capital of Srivijaya in its prime. Accordingly, it relates a story wherein Palembang-and-Temasek/Singapore are the rivals of Majapahit in Java, thus rendering the history of the Malay Archipelago a rivalry between an older, vanishing empire and a newly ascendant one.

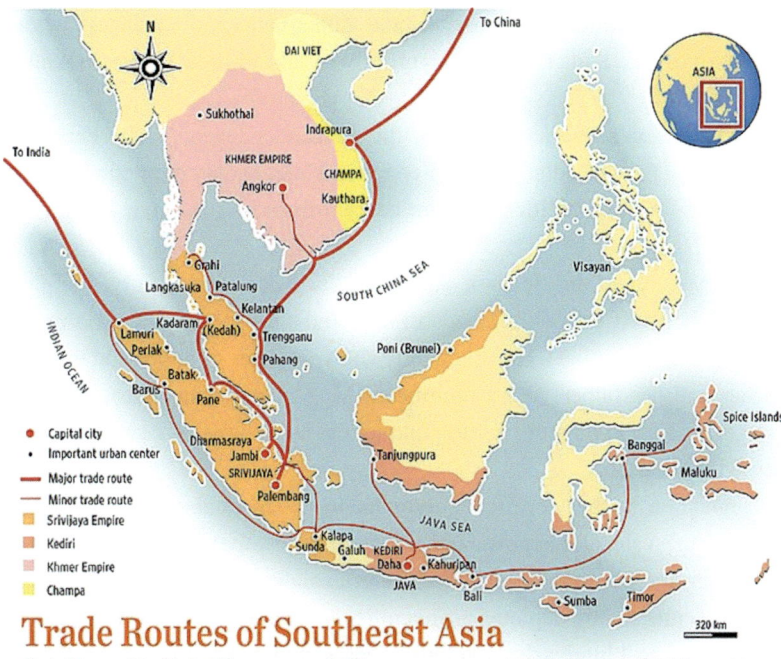

Trade Routes of Southeast Asia
Srivijaya, Kediri, Khmer, and Champa around XII to early XIII century
Gunawan

Fig. 8: Map of the Empire of Srivijaya

Royal Asiatic Society, London) is thought by the translator to derive from around 1612, when a *Bendahara* (chief minister, akin to a vizier) supposedly set down the text – though ultimately "we are still in the dark as to when exactly it was written" (xxiv–xxv, xi).[93]

Since my focus is globalism, rather than the history of the Malacca Sultanate, I teach the first six chapters of this thirty-one-chapter text, which highlight as their paramount focus the lively dispersal of peoples, and the creation of intercultural and geopolitical relations among them.

Those six chapters are replete with cultural, social, and historical detail, and attest an intense desire for connection to the deep past, and to the geopolitical cultures of the many Asias. Indeed, the *Annals* begins not in island Southeast Asia at all, but in India, with a union between a victorious Alexander the Great

---

[93] Some twenty-nine manuscripts are scattered in libraries in Indonesia, the UK, Netherlands, and Russia, with no critical edition yet available (xv). Originally dubbed the *Sulalatul Salatina* (Genealogy of the Sultans), the text is now by consensus known as the *Sejarah Melayu*, a historical compendium that proceeds more or less chronologically and features a long genealogy of kings and their chief ministers. For a concise discussion, see Derek Heng's chapter in *Teaching*. Page numbers refer to Brown's translation.

(here in his Arabic incarnation as Iskandar Zulkarnain) and a princess whose father's name, Raja Kida Hindi, eponymously recalls all India (India, in Arabic texts, is *al-Hind*).[94]

The Malay text's lively embrace of the Alexander legend underscores the global reach of the Macedonian world-conqueror's legendary reputation and the eagerness of far-flung polities to claim descent from him for their kings (see, especially, Ng).

In this version of his legend, Alexander/Iskandar successfully conquers India, and is given a beautiful and brilliant Indian princess with "no peer," "no equal," for wife (2, 3). He abundantly showers robes of honor and treasure upon her and her father, like a munificent Mughal potentate; then, after the marriage, goes off to do more world-conquering, but returns his new wife to her father, who misses her.

A connection to the world-conqueror having been established, the Indian princess births a son and begins a genealogy of begats that will link all successive rajas in her line to the great Iskandar/Alexander (4–5). Princesses, in the *Annals*, are consistently depicted as magnificent conduits for pedigreed descent from key historical luminaries and their empires. Some are named, and elaborately lauded, like this foremother who births Iskandar's/Alexander's Indian son, while others remain nameless and disappear from the narrative when their reproductive role is complete.

A keen-eyed student may notice from this early example of women-as-reproductive-conduits that the *Annals* has a different relationship to the body from most premodern texts. The way the princess knows she is pregnant is because "she did not menstruate," telling her father, "I have had no menses now for two months" (5). Ask your students: What other historical text(s) do they know of, where *menstruation* is so explicitly mentioned, and what do they make of this?

Beyond menstruation, bodily practices of an intimate, personal kind repeatedly appear. The Malayan slave Badang, a key figure in the premodern history of Singapore, acquires his superhuman strength when a demon (or jinn?) grants him a wish, but must eat the creature's *vomit* to gain his power (25). When Islam comes to the islands, a key character has a dream in which the Prophet Mohammad *spits* into his mouth, producing a fragrance like spikenard (32–33). A king of the Malacca Sultanate also has a dream about the Prophet and awakes to discover that he has been *circumcised* (43)! Proof – of authenticity, of the

---

[94] In the *Annals*, kings are called *raja*, testifying to the influence of Indic culture in island Southeast Asia, until the text announces the arrival of Islam, after which kings increasingly become *sultans*. Personal names and patronymics also become Islamized as the text registers the spread of Islam.

transference of power, of genuine change – must be visited on the body or involve intimate body-to-body relations.

A lack of prudery about the body and bodily practices is also clear from ceremonial bathing and purification in court rituals. The coronation of Sri Tri Buana/Sang Nila Utama,[95] the descendent of Iskandar/Alexander who becomes the new king at Palembang, along with his new queen, centrally involves a lustration ceremony, when the royal couple is publicly bathed, and clothed in new apparel before they are invested with the insignia of sovereignty (17).

Overall, global interconnections turn on folkloric, literary, and religious relations of multiple kinds, in a warp-and-weave of textual details. The insistence that Southeast Asia's kings are descended from Iskandar/Alexander, for instance, is vouched for by the behavior of descendants who act just like their famous ancestor. Raja Chulan, the descendant who fathers Sri Tri Buana, even repeats Alexander's legendary adventure of descending into the ocean in a premodern bathysphere – here, a "glass case," lowered by a golden chain (11).

Like the story of Jullanar and the Sea in the *Arabian Nights*, Chulan discovers there exists a well-populated undersea kingdom with a vast city and its own raja. Naturally, he is given a beautiful princess to marry, and he has three sons with her; when he decides to leave after three years – because he must go on to found a dynasty at "Bija Nagara" and remarry (sharp-eared students will instantly recognize Vijayanagar in this name) – Chulan leaves instructions for his sons to ascend to the surface when they grow to manhood, "so that the kingdom of Raja Iskandar Dzu'l-Karnain may not pass away but may continue for all time" (12).[96]

The *Annals'* ambitions are blazingly clear: Not only are the Malay kings genetically descended from Alexander the Great, but their legendary histories are also culturally interwoven with that glorious vehicle of Near Eastern story-making, the *Arabian Nights*. To emphasize this, Raja Chulan is flown out of the ocean by a "winged stallion," like the winged flying horse of the Third Dervish's Tale in the *Nights* story of the Porter and the Three Ladies.

The *Annals* never forgets, however, that Southeast Asia's ties to Iskandar are twinned with deep genetic, cultural, and historical ties to *India*. Again and again, as the *Annals* unfurls its stories, India is never far from textual attention.

---

[95] Like many in our premodern texts, this ruler is designated by different names. In Singapore's history books, he appears as Sang Nila Utama, rather than his other title, Sri Tri Buana (Lord of the Three Worlds). When he first appears, his personal name is announced as Nilatanam; after the king of Srivijayan Palembang abdicates in his favor, he receives the title of Sang Utama (14, 15).

[96] A Cambridge Element on how to teach the global Alexander legend is being prepared by Adam Miyashiro.

Elephants, betelnut, clothing, words from Indian languages, will all recall the vast interconnective tissue between India and the islands.[97]

Southeast Asia's rajas will also marry Indian princesses, including from Bija Nagara/Vijayanagar; and Southeast Asia's champions, like Singapore's strongman and war-chief, Badang, will compete with India's champions (and beat them handily in competitions of strength and strategy, attesting to successful *translatio imperii*).

The *Annals'* stories, then, map far-ranging relations for island Southeast Asia in a compressed and fluid timeline in which millennia or centuries are transmogrified into mere generations of royal descent: relations that unfold from the Mediterranean of the Iskandar/Alexander legend and the *Arabian Nights* to India; from India to Sumatra when Raja Chulan's sons emerge from their undersea home; thence to the Riau archipelago, after the youngest, most important son, Sang Nila Utama, is crowned ruler at the old imperial capital of Palembang; thereafter to the new capital of Temasek/Singapore that he founds, a capital that thrives and prospers, achieving world renown, and that must be defended from Majapahit in Java by his descendants; and eventually to the new Malacca Sultanate in peninsular Malaya, after Temasek/Singapore is lost, generations afterward, by its last king, Iskandar Shah.

When Islam is recorded as arriving in island Southeast Asia, and disseminates across the archipelago, yet another axis of globalism appears in the *Annals*.

By this point of the syllabus, students can see the whole massive network of global Islam traced across the texts of the semester: a spread that extends from Mali in West Africa, up the Volga to the Eurasian steppes, across North Africa/the Middle East/the Mediterranean, to India of the Ghaznavids, Gulbarga, and the Mughals, throughout island Southeast Asia, and all the way to China, where large Muslim mercantile communities are resident in the major port-cities (and murdered in Guangzhou during Huang Chao's rebellion, as Abu Zayd reports).

The *Annals'* mapping of all these global relationships, whether of a religious, historical, legendary, or sociocultural kind, is lively and engaging. One example is a charming episode narrating the emergence of Raja Chulan's sons from the undersea kingdom, when they've grown to adulthood, to establish the trajectory of *translatio imperii* from India to Sumatra. The story unfolds, not from the viewpoint of the young royal scions at all, but begins with two widows of

---

[97] Brown finds Telegu words being used for the garments (generically described as "sarongs") worn by Sri Tri Buana/Sang Nila Utama and his queen after their lustration ceremony – a dhoti made of silk, and a sari, both garments likely bejeweled (207 n.62).

Palembang, Wan Empok and Wan Malini, who plant rice (*padi*) on a hill called Bukit Si-Guntang Mahameru.[98]

One night, the widows see "a glow as of fire" on the hill. Hastening there fearfully, because it might be "the gleam of the gem on some great dragon's forehead," they climb the hill only to find that all the rice had "golden grain, leaves of silver and stems of gold alloy," and the entire crest of the hill "had turned into gold" (13–14).

There, the widows behold "three youths of great beauty" who were "adorned like kings and wore crowns studded with precious stones, and they rode upon white elephants" (14). The beautiful, brilliantly adorned youths assure the widows they are neither faery nor jinn but are "descended from Raja Iskandar Dzu'l-Karnain" (14).

As proof (proof matters to this text), they point to the transformation of the hilltop and rice, and relate the story of their ancestry from "the marriage of Raja Iskandar with Raja Kida Hindi's daughter and … the descent of Raja Chulan into the sea;" their crowns are the sign they are "of the stock of Raja Iskandar Dzu'l-Karnian" (14).[99]

Their Alexandrian lineage has now been mentioned three times, buttressing the assertion of a translation of rule. The widows are "filled with joy," and take the princes home with them – a poignant touch, since the widows' domestic circumstances are presumably humble and unworthy of hosting royal guests.

The entire episode is cinematic, with a delightfully staged *mise-en-scène*: Two old, widowed rice farmers suddenly encounter three unknown, dazzling, princely beings on a hill where everything has magicalized into gold and silver – a scene as worthy of the *Arabian Nights* as Hollywood. The contrast of youth with age, and opposite socioeconomic classes and stations in life, is psychologically satisfying; and the text, it seems, even cares what happens to the widows: "Wan Empok and Wan Malini became rich because of their meeting with the princes" (14).

News about the royal youths spreads, and the king of Palembang, Demang Lebar Daun, goes to the widows' home to meet the princes, whereupon "every ruler from every part of the country" follows suit, and people decide to make the

---

[98] Bukit Siguntang or Seguntang is a hill in Palembang associated with Srivijaya, while *Mahameru* is the sacred mountain, Mount Meru, of Hindu-Buddhist cosmology. The conjunction of names thus magnifies the symbolic import of this royal manifestation.

[99] The existence of undersea kingdoms notwithstanding, textual realism seems to matter to the *Annals*, since we see Raja Chulan earlier preparing for this moment, by leaving a commemorative rock with "a record in writing in the Hindustani language" and a treasure hoard, at the location of his return to land, for the time when "a prince of my line shall possess this treasure … who shall make all the lands below the wind subject to him" (12). The "wind/s" mentioned repeatedly in this text are the monsoons, and the "land below the wind/s" is thus island Southeast Asia.

eldest youth the raja of Menangkabau, the next eldest the raja of Tanjong Pura, while the youngest ascends to the throne at Palembang when Demang Lebar Daun decides to abdicate in his favor, and become the youth's chief minister instead (14–15).

The widows, moreover, are not forgotten. They possess a silvery white cow, which spews *foam* from its mouth, from which a human being emerges, who bestows Sang Utama with a new title, "Sri Tri Buana," Lord of the Three Worlds, addressing him as "Sri Maharaja" – the radiant, supreme king of the land (15). This new king becomes "famous as a ruler; and all mankind, male and female, came from every part of the country to pay their homage to him" (15).

Yet another story echoing the *Arabian Nights* follows: Sri Tri Buana takes one beautiful princess after another for his consort, but each, "when she slept with the king," is stricken with chloasma the next morning, so he abandons thirty-nine princesses in succession (15).[100] The king then asks for the hand of his new chief minister's daughter, Wan Sendari, whose beauty "had no equal in those days" (15–16).

This memento from the *Nights'* frame tale serves a different purpose, however, from Shahrazad's story. Here, the chief minister uses the occasion to bind the new king and all his royal descendants to a covenant. Under the terms of the pact, the king and his descendants must treat the minister and *his* descendants fairly, in return for their loyalty, and must never disgrace or revile them with evil words, though grave offenses remain punishable by death, in accordance with law.

The king agrees, adding a self-serving proviso: "your descendants shall never for [the] rest of time be disloyal to my descendants, even if my descendants oppress them and behave evilly" (16). The minister carefully agrees, but in words that reestablish *causal priority*: "But if your descendants depart from the terms of the pact, then so will mine" (16). The *Annals* sets down these terms as an irrevocable covenant:

> And that is why it has been granted by Almighty God to Malay rulers that they shall never put their subjects to shame, and that those subjects however greatly they offend shall never be bound or hanged or disgraced with evil words. If any ruler puts a single one of his subjects to shame, that shall be a sign that this kingdom will be destroyed by Almighty God (16).

The precautions taken by Demang Lebar Daun are one example of the wisdom and prudence of chief ministers in the *Annals*, a text that may have been composed

---

[100] Medical literature indicates that chloasma or melasma, which darkens the skin patchily, is a condition that can afflict women in pregnancy, because of hormonal changes. It seems unlikely the king is discarding princesses because they have become pregnant by him overnight, but the *Annals*, true to form, remains attentive to intimate bodily conditions, as a pretext to build dramatic momentum toward finding the right princess, and sealing a match with her.

or set down by a chief minister. Over and over, in the *Annals*, chief ministers' wisdom, sagacity, and courage save imprudent and fatuous kings from disaster. The canny intelligence of chief ministers in India, China, and Southeast Asia, wins wars, prevents invasions, and ransoms kings from captivity; ungrateful kings who do not appreciate their ministers tend to come to a poor end in the *Annals*.

This compact binding the ruler of the land and his descendants, negotiated over a bride, therefore inserts a foreshadowing explanation for the eventual loss of Singapore to Java, when a royal descendant of Sri Tri Buana behaves badly over a woman, and the woman's father, who is one of the ruler's chief men, betrays all to the Majapahit empire, when the terms of the covenant between ruler and ministerial subject utterly break down.

Wan Sendari does not develop melasma when she sleeps with the king, indicating she is the prefect consort. Their ceremonial lustration requires the building of a seven-tier bathing pavilion with five spires, as well as forty days and nights of feasting, drinking, and entertainment, the investiture festivities being attended by princes, ministers, courtiers, heralds, war-chiefs and all the people, and celebrated with music, food, and herds of slaughtered animals.

Thereafter, Sri Tri Buana sets out to found a new city, on ships crowding the seas: a golden ship for the menfolk, a silver one for the queen, each minister and war-chief with their own craft, and the fleet so vast, their masts "were like a forest of trees, their pennons and streamers were like driving clouds and the state umbrellas of the Rajas like cirrus" (17–18).

This, it seems, is how the courts of island worlds travel: in a vast fleet of "royal yachts, ships for sleeping, ships for the menfolk, wherries that were paddled, kitchen boats, dug-outs for fishing with the casting-net and floating bath-houses … with a countless host of escorting vessels" so that "the sea seemed to be nothing but ships" (19, 18).

The road to the founding of Singapore first leads to the island of Bintang ("Bentan") in the Riau-Lingga archipelago, where a queen, Wan Sri Benian, or Sakidar Shah (her name in another tradition), welcomes and adopts Sri Tri Buana as her son, in a diplomatic extension of manufactured kin relations that here serves political relations, and becoming so fond of him that she installs him as her successor (18–29).

Next, leaving Bintang,[101] the court arrives at Tanjong Bemian, and, while the queen and her womenfolk picnic and gather shellfish, the king follows a deer he

---

[101] Students of European romances will notice not only how similar court festivities are around the world, but also how similar the excuses of courtly men are, when they want to go adventuring. After being at Bintang for a while, the king announces he needs to travel for hunting, and, despite Sakidar Shah reminding him of the ample game in her land, he insists, "If I am not permitted to go, then I shall die" (19).

is hunting, climbs a rock and sights a land with a beach with "sand so white that it looked like a sheet of cloth" (19).[102] Intrigued, the king is told the name of the island is Temasek; and he decides to sail there. Enroute, however, a storm arises, his ship fills with water, and the boatswain announces "it is because of the crown of kingship that the ship is foundering" since all else has been thrown overboard to lighten the ship (20).[103]

Unhesitatingly, the king flings his crown overboard: "the storm abated, and the ship regained her buoyancy and was rowed to land" (20). Scholars understand this act of crown-discarding as the moment at which the old sovereignty of Srivijaya is symbolically given up, superseded by a new sovereignty expressing renewal and resurgence, when a brand-new capital is founded in Singapore by a youthful new king, Sri Tri Buana.

The naming of that new capital is a story every school child in Singapore knows. Arriving in Temasek, the king sees a strange beast, "strong and active in build," with a red body, a black head, and a white breast, and nobody can tell him what it is. His chief minister, who had been the old king at the old Srivijayan capital, tells him, "in ancient times it was a lion that had that appearance" (20).

The new king then decides to rename Temasek *Singapura* – Sanskrit for "lion city" – and establish his capital there: "And Singapura became a great city, to which foreigners resorted in large numbers so that the fame of the city and its greatness spread throughout the world" (21).[104]

Sri Tri Buana dies in the fullness of time, and is buried, along with his faithful chief minister, at Bukit Larangan ("Forbidden Hill," later renamed Fort Canning, by the British Colonial Administration) in Singapore.[105]

Majapahit, whose king had married the daughter of Sri Tri Buana's elder brother who had been given Tanjong Pura to rule, soon tests the royal successor, Sri Tri Buana's eldest son. Majapahit's king is puissant – "So great was his kingdom that every prince in the land of Java was subject to him, as was half of

---

[102] "Excavations carried out in 2003 by Professor John Miksic and his team in the National University of Singapore have in fact revealed the existence of a layer of pure white sand ... dating back to the 14th century" in southern Singapore (https://thelongnwindingroad.wordpress.com/2023/09/30/the-case-of-the-missing-beach/).

[103] From Ibn Shahriyar, students know this is what you do in a storm: lighten the ship by throwing everything overboard.

[104] That this is the latest stage in Srivijayan *translatio imperii* is highlighted when the king sends to Bintang for "men, elephants and horses without number" because he intends to reign from Singapura henceforth (20). So, half a planet away from Mali, whose capital, Niani, is the center of the world, Sri Tri Buana's capital, Singapura, in Southeast Asia, also becomes the center of the world.

[105] Excavations at Fort Canning have found gold jewelry with gemstones that were likely royal possessions (see Fig.9). The artifacts are now displayed at the National Museum of Singapore (https://www.roots.gov.sg/Collection-Landing/listing/1010123 and see Ong).

Fig. 9: Royal gold jewelry excavated from Bukit Larangan/Fort Canning in Singapore

the princes of Nusantara [i.e. the Malay Archipelago]" – because in the fourteenth century, Majapahit is an ascendant empire indeed (22).

A fascinating contest of insults and boasts is exchanged between the envoys of both polities through gifts of heavy-handed symbolism that vaunt the unique talents of each populace, after which Majapahit invades with "a hundred ships and small craft without number" (23). A great battle ensues, where on "either side many were killed and the ground flowed with blood," but ends with the Javanese returning home without success (23). Singapore does not fall.

Instead, premodern Singapore enters its heyday. The king of Bija Nagara/ Vijayanagar gives his beautiful daughter as wife for the Singapore ruler's son, thereby directly linking Singapore with a famed Indian empire. That son in turn ascends to kingship on his sire's death (24). The relationship between the old world and the new one, proves ineluctably competitive, however; and a champion is sent by India to test the mettle of Singapore's champions: but Badang, the former slave from Malaya with superhuman strength, is now a war-chief of Singapore, and easily bests the Indian champion in feats of strength.

Their capstone contest involves a massive boulder, which the Indian champion fails to lift, but which Badang handily lifts and hurls (see Fig. 10 for a reenactment), landing the boulder by the mouth of the Singapore River (27).

Believed originally to span three meters in height and width, this boulder, today known as the Singapore Stone, became a casualty of the British Empire, when it was blown to pieces in the nineteenth century by the British Colonial Administration and used as building material for British living quarters and

Fig. 10: A simulation of Badang lifting the Singapore Stone, National Day Parade, Singapore, 2016

fortifications. A fragment of the boulder fortuitously survives, bearing an inscription: fifty lines in the Kawi script (Old Javanese) which have yet to be fully deciphered; that slab of rock is today an exhibit at the National Museum of Singapore.

Badang also stretches a chain across the Singapore River,[106] to act "as a boom and restrict the passage of ships in and out," and accomplishes other legendary feats, including launching a ship twelve fathoms long that even a few hundred men could not launch, and beating a champion sent by the king of Perlak in an informal trial of strength where Badang's tact and diplomacy skillfully averts war (26–29).

When Singapore does fall, then, it is not because of military weakness or the deficiencies of its war-chiefs, but because a feckless king makes a foolish mistake.

The tragedy is prepared for by first showing us the poor behavior of kings. For instance, the *Annals* has it that Singapore was once attacked by swordfish that speared and killed many people, until a boy cannily suggests that a palisade of tree trunks ("banana stems") be erected, so that the pointed bills of the fish would be stuck in the palisade. The suggestion saves Singapore, but the king of

---

[106] The British Colonial Administration reports the existence of this chain across the Singapore River when the British arrived in the nineteenth century.

the time has the boy killed, in case such an imaginative child should grow up to be "a clever man" who might prove dangerous (40).[107]

That king's son, Iskandar Shah, proves even more unwise than his father, when, as king, he decides to punish one of his favorite concubines, a very beautiful woman, because of hearsay attributed by the *Annals* to "the king's womenfolk," who "spoke ill of her" and accuse her of "misconduct." The accused woman's father is no ordinary subject, but a Treasury official holding the title Sang Ranjuna Tapa: Nonetheless, Iskandar Shah has the woman "publicly exposed at one end of the market," punishing her in sexualized terms, to the anger of her father (41).[108]

The intimation in this episode, it seems, is that the king's womenfolk (out of jealousy?) have accused the beautiful concubine of *sexual* misconduct, for which the king then devises a sexualized punishment: having her stripped naked, and exposed to public gawking and humiliation.

The father avenges his disgraced daughter by writing to Majapahit and offering to aid an invasion, and Majapahit responds by sending a fleet of 300 ships, "together with countless galleys, commissariat craft and dugouts" and 200,000 Javanese fighting men (41). After days of battle, "Sultan Iskandar Shah ordered the Treasury to issue rice for the provisioning of the troops but Sang Ranjuna Tapa replied that there was no rice left" (41). At dawn, the vengeful father opens the gates of the fortified city, and "so many were killed on either side that blood flowed like a river in spate and flooded the fort of Singapura on the sea shore" (41).

"And the men of Singapura were defeated, and Sultan Iskandar Shah fled" (41). The *Annals* follows the defeated sultan into peninsular Malaya, till he arrives at Malacca, where he decides to stay and build a new kingdom. The rest of chapter 6 then narrates the establishment of the new court, with lists of sumptuary decrees, ceremonial rites and rituals, diplomatic procedures, and the titles and duties of the chief ministers – the *Bendahara*, *Temenggong*, and *Laksamana* – in what will become the Malacca Sultanate, and the following chapters narrate the Sultanate's history up to Portuguese colonization in 1511.[109]

---

[107] This same king earlier had a man put to death because of sexual jealousy, when his queen witnessed the man's prowess in magic: an episode perhaps foreshadowing his son's sexual jealousy, which leads to the fall of Singapore (40).

[108] We are not told if the father believes in his daughter's innocence, just that he is outraged by the nature of the punishment: "Even if my daughter is guilty of misconduct, let her merely be put to death, why humiliate her like this?" (41). In one cinematic portrayal of the fall of Singapore, based on the *Annals*, the young woman is in love with and committed to someone, but Iskandar Shah opposes the lovers and wants to conscript the woman into his harem.

[109] In another tradition, Iskandar Shah is Parameswara, the latest descendant of the royal Srivijayan bloodline, who issues from the Melayu Kingdom to become the founder of Singapore, loses

In the fall of Singapore, then, *women* are blamed, for accusing one of their own, a concubine who is a king's favorite, with the feckless king then arranging a particularly nasty punishment for his ex-favorite that outrages her father to the point that he sets in motion actions that result in the destruction of the kingdom. The old compact between king and officials, agreed upon by the first ruler of Singapore and his chief minister to ensure fair treatment on both sides of a power equation, breaks down, we see, because of the calumny of a woman by other women, and a king's design of a humiliating punishment for the calumniated.[110]

Students will be familiar with gender accusations that blame women for the fall of kingdoms and empires, of course, from literary texts of many kinds, in many eras. But if they are disheartened at the portrayal of women in the texts of the semester, our ending the semester with the Mongols will soften their dismay a little.

8 The Globalism of *Pax Mongolica*: Teaching the *Secret History of the Mongols* and Marco Polo-Rustichello of Pisa's *Description of the World*

The globalism of the Mongols is so well known today that it's hardly necessary to argue for the importance of teaching the *Secret History of the Mongols* in a global curriculum.[111] Thanks to the myth of Genghis Khan's widely circulating DNA in the populations of the world, innumerable popular books and academic studies on Mongols, and increasing attention to the importance of *Pax Mongolica* for trade, the arts, technology, religion, and culture, fascination with Mongols is surely on the rise.[112]

None of this is surprising, given the reach of an empire whose invasions stretched from Poland, Bohemia, Hungary, Iran, and Iraq in the west, to China

---

Singapore to Majapahit, and founds the Malacca Sultanate. In a Malay court, the *Bendahara* is the chief minister, like a vizier, the *Temenggong* is the minister of home affairs, whose duties include security and the maintenance of order, and the *Laksamana* is the admiral of the navy.

[110] Of the global texts in my syllabus, the *Malay Annals* is likely to be least familiar to readers. I've thus gone into some detail to suggest guidelines on how to approach and teach the *Annals*.

[111] Page numbers refer to de Rachewiltz's open-access online and print translation, but readers are urged to consult Atwood's Penguin translation as an alternative teaching text. Atwood, like de Rachewiltz's three-volume print translation, has a comprehensive introduction, appendices, maps, family genealogies, and copious notes, especially on philological matters. Atwood also has a glossary of names, while de Rachewiltz has a massive index for locating people, events, places, etc., mentioned in the text. Both have extensive explanatory notes that furnish ample help in teaching.

[112] I follow the familiar older spelling of Genghis Khan's name (rather than *Cinggis Qan*), and the names of other figures in the *Secret History*, and omit diacritical marks, for ease of reading. Timothy May is authoring an Element on the spread of food and drink, or what he calls "the Chinggisid Exchange" – a precursor of the "Columbian Exchange."

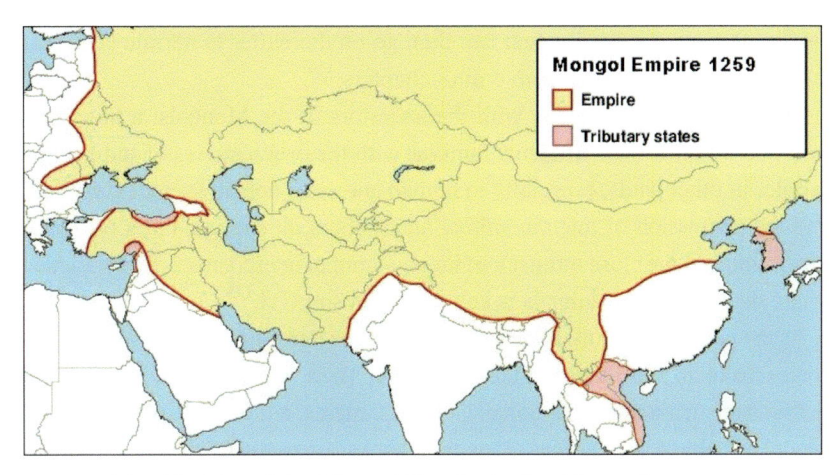

Fig. 11: Map of the Mongol Empire in the thirteenth century

and Korea in the east, subsumed Russia in the north, and encompassed Tibet, Burma, and Vietnam to the south, with even island Southeast Asia paying tribute to the Mongols (see Fig. 11).

Teaching *The Secret History of the Mongols*

The extraordinary Mongolian epic known as *The Secret History of the Mongols* is the only "genuine . . . native account" of the life and deeds of Genghis Khan and the genealogy and history of his "Golden Family," who are the epic's intended audience (xxv). This thirteenth-century text also, of course, narrates the origins, genealogies, and interrelated histories of the most important personages, clans, and societies on the steppe that intertwine with the history of Genghis Khan.[113]

A productive approach for teaching the *Secret History* might be to ask: What were the *early conditions* that allowed for Genghis Khan's emergence and survival in the first place, hence enabling his later empire with its renowned globalism, to have a chance to begin at all?

Approaching the epic in this way foregrounds the important roles of *women* in the text. It also allows us to concentrate on teaching the first three chapters to undergraduates, constituting about 45 percent of the numbered sections in this dense twelve-chapter text, since these are the chapters establishing the values, attitudes, and practices that are foundational for all

---

[113] For the *Secret History*'s compiler, and the linguistic, authorial, editorial, transmissional, and translational history of the manuscript, and its relation to the *Yuan Shih*, China's official history of the Yuan dynasty, see de Rachewiltz xxv–lix and Atwood's introduction and afterword.

the later events, so that the text can then go on thereafter to narrate conquest after conquest in the successive nine chapters.[114]

The *Secret History* begins with the ancestors of the Mongols: a blue-grey wolf and a fallow deer. Students familiar with the origin stories of Indigenous peoples in other lands, especially in nomad and semi-nomad societies, will not find the possession of totemic animal ancestors at all strange, but a powerful way to catch at the close intimacy of human–animal interconnection in societies where dependency on animals is key to human survival.[115]

As the narration begins a line of begats, we see that when persons are named, horses make an appearance at the same time: There was such-and-such a man, and he had such-and-such a horse. Geldings, mares, equines of all colors, with mangy or bobbed tails, stripes along their backs, are routinely described, so that family, clan, and tribal wealth are seen to be reckoned by the number of horses and herds possessed.

Mongols, of course, not only ride, but also drink, eat, and wear their horses. Kumiss, fermented mares' milk, is a food staple; horse hide becomes shoes, cuirasses, clothing; horsehair becomes rope; horse guts are the strings of the horsehead fiddle; horse dung is useful for fuel. No part of the animal is wasted: Mongols clearly respect their steeds but do not sentimentalize or romanticize them, as knights do in European romances. Life on the steppe is so harsh, the papal legate John of Plano Carpini says in his *Hystoria Mongalorum*, that Mongols eat just about everything that lives, including the placenta of mares and even lice (*Race* 294).

Students can be asked to consider the roles of animals-as-surrogates in the semester's epics, such as the owls in *Sundiata* who carry taunts, boasts, and threats between the warring Sunjata and Sumaoro, or Bodoncar's hawk in the *History*, who catches prey for him, which he and the bird share, so that both are able to survive on the steppes.

Sharp-eyed students will notice that grain scarcely makes an appearance in *this* epic: No heaps of rice are harvested here for celebrations, but roasted fowl, deer and game, field animals, fish, and herds are what feed people – who, in

---

[114] I ask graduate students to read all twelve chapters, but undergraduates usually find the first three so dense, and opaque, that requiring them to read the entire epic is impractical. Fortunately, the first three are the epic's foundational chapters, containing 126 sections. Concomitantly, watching Sergei Bodrov's *Mongol* helps students visualize landscapes, customs, and clothing on the steppe, though they should be warned of the liberties the film takes with plotlines and characters. Departing from earlier translations, Atwood's divides his into eight chapters, and forty-four "sub-chapters," but retains the same numbering for sections, ending with section 281, not 282.

[115] "[I]n the early legend of Mongol origins [these] are real animals, as in the mythology of the ancient Turks whose totemic ancestor was likewise a wolf. However, in the later Mongol tradition they become a human couple" (1: 224). Atwood leaves the "ambiguity" of animal or human origins "unresolved" (221 n.1).

desperate circumstances, will also eat roots, bulbs, and leaves. The lack of plant agriculture and the reliance on animal husbandry and transhumance helps bring home the realities of nomad societies, where even alcoholic beverages come from animals, not plants.

The steppes constitute an exceptionally harsh world. Here is an environment where not only martial skill and violence, but equally resilience, courage, determination, pragmatism, and ingenuity – qualities possessed in abundance by women – are the prime strengths. Sociality is all-important, too, and despite divisions in families, especially among brothers, the imperative of companionship and allies is an overriding condition for survival. To be cast off from society, and alone on the steppes, is to face probable death.

Key values surface early in the epic and are often performed by the example of iconic women. Earliest among these is Genghis' ancestress, Alan Qoa ("Alan the Fair"), who, after two sons with her late husband, births three more sons when she is a widow. Accused of sexual impropriety, she declares that the three sons are the result of visitations by a celestial being, a resplendent yellow (i.e., golden) man who came to her nightly through the smoke hole of her yurt, departing on a moonbeam or sun's ray as a yellow (golden) dog (I: 4).[116]

Alan Qoa's extraordinary explanation for the origins of her seemingly illegitimate sons is trusted absolutely and without question, signaling this remarkable ancestress's exceptionality, and authority.[117] Her words then constitute the basis of the future Genghis' perceived favor from heaven: A woman has *ab origine* conferred celestial ancestry, and heaven's mandate, upon the future world-conqueror (I: 264).

As importantly, this foundational ancestress lays down instruction to her five sons in a dictate whose truth will echo down the generations. She teaches them that five arrows, bound together, cannot be broken, whereas a single arrow breaks easily, a lesson that survival is only possible if an individual is part of a group that holds together.[118] Positioned early in the epic, her instruction casts

---

[116] De Rachewiltz discusses the importance of yellow, the color of gold, in the Mongol color system. Genghis Khan's family is the "Golden Family," and khans have golden pavilions and *gers*/yurts (I: 264), symbolizing "power and leadership" and "royal authority" (I: 263). Yellow/gold is thus synecdochic of the royal and imperial, whereas black signifies what is common or of lower status (I: 265). White is "a sign of wealth, nobility and rank" (I: 265), an auspicious color betokening "luck and a happy destiny," perhaps because it recalls light and radiance (I: 328). Blue is the color of the sky, "Eternal Heaven," the domain of the steppe deity Tengri, "identified in [Turkic and Mongolic] cultures with the Supreme Power governing the destiny of all creatures" (I: 225).

[117] By contrast, we see the paternity of children by other husbandless widows being doubted (e.g., I: 8).

[118] Her allegory is traditional among "nomadic peoples of eastern Europe and Asia . . . long before the Mongols," and appears among Aesop's fables (I: 262).

a long shadow, and Genghis' career will see him prize loyalty as a sine qua non among followers, even as he himself is disloyal to allies only after he has the strategic strength of numbers.

The woman who looms largest in the foundational chapters of the *History*, however, is Genghis' mother, Hoelun, who is awarded the honorific, *Lady* Hoelun, then *Mother* Hoelun, early in the epic.[119] Her abduction by Yisugei, Genghis' father, ripping her from her betrothed, a Merkit, is a chilling reminder of female vulnerability, bride-capture being commonplace on the steppe (I: 11–12). We see from an earlier abduction initiated by Alan Qoa's son Bodoncar, that even *pregnant* women are not exempt from forcible capture that conscripts them as wives and concubines for their captors (I: 7–8).[120] But if bride-capture – like raiding – is part of the socioeconomy of the steppe, we also witness Hoelun's formidable resilience, as her actions secure the survival of the future Genghis Khan.

When Temujin, the future Genghis, is a boy of nine, his father Yisuge is poisoned by vengeful Tatars with whom Yisuge incautiously socializes on his way home after having found Temujin a bride among the Onggirat (I: 16).[121] With the paterfamilias dead, the family's kin and tribe abandon Hoelun, her co-wife, their combined seven children, and at least one elderly servant, who must fend for themselves in an inhospitable environment without the safety of a large protective group of kin and community.[122] Nonetheless, raising aloft the stand-ard of her late husband's clan, Hoelun bravely rides forth to bring back her

---

[119] Atwood translates these as "Madame O'elun" and "Madame Mother," "Noble Madame," and "Motherly Madame" (10, 17, 18, *passim*).

[120] Genghis and his Golden Family descend from this Bodoncar, the youngest son underestimated by his brothers as a "fool and a half-wit" when Alan Qoa dies, and who goes off to survive on his own with the help of a female hawk (I: 5–6). Socializing with "a band of people" and drinking kumiss with them, Bodoncar suggests to his elder brother, who comes to bring him home, that they attack those same friendly folk because they lacked a leader and thus "are people easy to capture" (I: 7). The five sons of Alan Qoa attack "and robbed those people, and in this way got enough livestock, people to serve them, and a place to live" (I: 7). Bodoncar's earlier subaltern status, and his later unprovoked, ruthless opportunism, foreshadow his famous descendant's own hapless beginnings and ruthless opportunism.

[121] "Genghis Khan" is the world-conqueror's assumed name, *Temujin* being his birth-name. Yisuge's poisoning is not the first example of the blood feuds and rounds of vengeance that are presented as commonplace in steppe societies. The imperative as well as the danger of sociality and hospitality, in Bodoncar's and Yisuge's examples, are also signaled as intrinsic to steppe customs.

[122] Focusing on Hoelun's heroism, the text forgets to say whether Yisuge's "foster-son" Monglik is present – an adult male, of twenty to thirty years at this time, who had been tasked by Yisuge to protect his family after his death (I: 339–340). The family's old male servant, Caraqa (Monglik's biological father), who was speared by the departing tribe, also may have been present (I: 16). So intent is the textual focus on Hoelun and her sons, Yisuge's other wife, and the family's old female servant, are not mentioned either, but reappear when they are kidnapped by the Merkit, along with Borte, Temujin's future wife (I: 31).

Fig. 12: A high-ranking married Mongol woman's *boqta*, a symbol of
rank and authority

people, but only half return with her, and these folks do not stay, but abandon her
family again.

A long, beautiful poem follows, where the *History* sings of Hoelun's courage
and tenacity in protecting her small family. She girds herself with the symbols of
her authority, her *boqta*, a tall, elaborate headdress worn by married women of
high rank (see Fig. 12), and, tightening her belt (another symbol of authority)
and hoisting up her skirts, poignantly begins the process of gathering humble

famine foods – crab apples and bird cherries, roots, wild garlic, wild onion, lily bulbs, and leeks – to feed her family, while her sons fish for "mean and paltry fish" (I: 19–20).[123]

In this environment of terrible scarcity and precarity, Temujin and his brother Qasar horrifically commit fratricide, killing their half-brother Bekter, the son of Yisuge's other wife, over the pretext of quarreling over a dace and a lark (I: 20–21). Despite (or because of) textual restraint in narrating this episode – students can be asked to compare the *History*'s spareness with the *Vinland Sagas'* – pathos pervades the episode.

Bekter, who is guarding the family's small herd of nine horses, suspects he is going to be killed, when he sees Temujin and Qasar stealthily approach. Quietly, he reminds his half-brothers of their precarious circumstances, their inability to avenge their abandonment, and how alone they are. Summoning up the memory of Alan Qoa's allegory of the five arrows, he asks why his brothers consider him "a lash in the eye, a thorn in the mouth," when they have "no friend but [their] shadow ... no whip but [their] horse's tale."[124] He pleads, not for his life, but for them to spare his brother Belgutei, then, sitting cross-legged, awaits their arrows (I: 20–21, I: 367–368).

De Rachewiltz suggests that this fratricide, so expressive of ruthlessness at a tender age, strategically rids Temujin of a future rival in his family (I: 347). Nonetheless, Hoelun excoriates her sons for the sibling murder: "You ... have destroyed life!" (I: 21, I: 368). "Hoelun's Lament" – "a beautiful and powerful piece of early Mongol poetry" (I: 368) – recalls how Temujin emerged from Hoelun's womb clutching a clot of blood – that is, with blood on his hands, a foretaste of mercilessness (I: 21).[125] Likening her son to a savage, uncontrollable animal – a panther, lion, dragon-snake, gerfalcon, wolf, jackal, tiger – and unnatural beasts, Hoelun's tongue-lashing crescendos, "You have destroyed!" (I: 21). "Citing old sayings, / Quoting ancient words, [Hoelun] mightily reviled her sons" (I: 22).[126]

We are not told what Temujin learns from Hoelun's tongue-lashing, but as an adult, we see him turn to his mother for her counsel, when he must decide if he

---

[123] On the symbolism of the *boqta* and the belt, and the sacral power symbolized by the clan's war standard, see I: 352–353 and I: 350.

[124] Compare this haunting saying with the Kurds' *we have no friend but the mountain*.

[125] "The story of the new-born child holding a clot of blood ... is an ancient Asiatic folklore theme ... portending the advent of a fierce and merciless conqueror" (I: 321). Timur Lenkh ("Tamerlane" to the West) was likewise born "with blood on his hand(s)" (I: 321).

[126] "Pounding in the past times' words and echoing the elders' words, she accused them fiercely" (Atwood 19).

and his men should follow or leave his *anda*, Jamuqa, and Jamuqa's men (I: 45–46).[127]

Once Temujin's conquests begin, we see Hoelun in a new role, adopting and raising children from conquered tribes, a process that transforms the children of the defeated into future loyal retainers for her son, her first adoptee being "a little boy of five with fire in his eyes," after Temujin's first conquest (I: 43).

Hoelun's impact thus continues after her son is no longer a child. In chapter 10 of the *History*, when Temujin harshly mistreats and humiliates his brother Qasar, Hoelen travels all night to her sons, and again in fury excoriates her eldest (I: 168–170). The text says, "surprised by the mother descending upon him," Genghis "became afraid of her" (I: 169).

Again, issuing a tongue-lashing in verse, Hoelun performs a dramatic gesture that students may be familiar with from depictions of furious mothers in medieval European literature: She bares her breasts to remind her sons they have nursed from the same maternal breasts and share the same mother (I: 169). Meant to shame misbegotten sons into better behavior, this maternal breast-bearing and fury have the desired effect: Genghis confesses, "I was afraid of mother getting so angry and really became frightened; and I felt shame and was really abashed" (I: 170).[128]

Borte, Temujin's first (and chief) wife is another crucial personage who lays the groundwork for his early survival. When we first meet her, she and Temujin are characterized in identical terms: Both are children radiant with promise, bearing light in their face, and fire in their eyes (I: 14–15).

A year older, Borte is from a tribe who sees their daughters as their chief strength, and a charming poem tells of how the Onggirat do not bother with power struggles or strive "for dominion," because their daughters are so much in demand that the tribe's safety is ensured by their women who become khatuns and the tribe's protectors (I: 14–15).[129]

---

[127] In yet another example of how fictive kinships are shown in premodern texts to serve important ends – cementing political, military, or trade relations – Mongol men have sworn brotherhoods, with a boon companion called an *anda*, to forge loyalties and ensure assistance. The degree of closeness between *andas* is debated, but "There is no doubt that the *anda*-relationship was a form of very close friendship and indissoluble alliance" (I: 395–396).

[128] Genghis immediately ceases and desists, but he is now a successful, ruthless conqueror and no longer a child, and continues *secretly* to punish Qasar (I: 170).

[129] Atwood says this pacific characterization is retroactive: "up until Chinggis Khan's unification of Mongolia, the Qonggirat were active players in power politics ... with the unification, the Qonggirat acquired their identity as the classic *quda* or marriage-ally people" (227–228 n.54). In Polo-Rustichello, Kublai Khan's imperial harem is recruited from this same Onggirat ("Kunggurat") tribe. De Rachewiltz tells us Mongols prefer a steppe aristocrat's wife to be older: Since girls mature faster than boys, the reasoning goes, she can initiate her husband into sexual relations and "be able to guide and counsel him in worldly matters" (I: 332), adding that guidance and counsel are precisely Borte's role with Temujin later (I: 332–333).

Marriage to Borte brings a treasure indispensable for cementing a key alliance at the first stage of Temujin's military career. Borte's bridal gift – a wedding present from her mother to Hoelun – is a magnificent black sable coat. The first thing of real value the family possesses is thus brought by a woman (I: 30). Temujin suborns the sable, and presents it to his father's *anda*, the Ong Khan, leader of the powerful Kereit tribe, who is so pleased with the gift that he breaks into poetry and promises to restore Temujin's people to him (I: 30).[130]

Later, when Borte is abducted by the Merkit in revenge for Yisuge's earlier abduction of Hoelun, the Ong Khan proves indispensable, throwing his forces behind Temujin and Jamuqa, Temujin's *anda*, to restore Borte and the other abducted women of Temujin's family. This crucial military alliance – the first of many – lays the ground for Temujin's acquisition of enough forces and men to consolidate the first step in his military campaigns.

The next step is again secured by Borte. After the conquest of the Merkit, Borte intervenes when Temujin asks his mother for advice as to whether he and his men should remain with Jamuqa's forces, with whom they have been traveling for a year and a half. "Before Mother Hoelun could utter a sound, Lady Borte" interjects to argue for leaving at once, and traveling by night (I: 46).

"They all approved of the words of Lady Borte," and Temujin and his men set off on their own (I: 46). This decisive break will bring challenges and setbacks, but it is also essential for Temujin's emergence from under the shadow of Jamuqa, to become a leader in his own right, able to command the obedience of troops, and even to recruit those of Jamuqa's men who decide to follow him. More men arrive, and Temujin is made khan – becoming, now, *Genghis Khan*.[131]

As the third chapter of the *Secret History* concludes, students will have amply witnessed the decisive roles played by Mongol women, and will be less surprised to see, in other texts about the Mongols, women acting as rulers, regents, governors, ambassadors, and advisors in the Mongol Empire.

In the Franciscan John of Plano Carpini's *Hystoria Mongalorum*, students see that John, the papal ambassador from the Latin West, gains access to the Great Khan Guyuk, Genghis' grandson, only after he has first met with Guyuk's mother, Toreghana Khatun, and has been checked out by this matriarch,

---

[130] "The reason why the sable coat, i.e. the bride's present … was given to the Ong Khan is because … the young Temujin needed … a powerful ally and protector, and Ong Khan was the obvious person" (I: 396).

[131] Borte's counsel is again decisive in chapter 10, when she counsels another strategic break (I: 171–172).

a wily Naiman empress-dowager who herself ruled as Great Khatun for five years after her husband's death, and before her son's ascension (*Race* 298–299).

John also reports how powerful Sorghagtani Beki ("Sorocan") was – the Kereit wife of Genghis' youngest son Tolui, and mother of the Great Khans Mongke, and Kublai, and the Ilkhan Hulegu (*Race* 298, 387).

Later, when Louis IX of France sends the Dominican, Andrew of Longjumeau, to Guyuk with letters and lavish gifts, Andrew finds Guyuk deceased, and his widow, Oghul Gamish, ruling in his place. It is therefore a woman – Jean de Joinville in his *Histoire de Saint Louis* mistakes her for a man – who takes the French king's gifts for tribute, and haughtily orders Louis to keep paying tribute (*Race* 299).

The famous pragmatism of the Mongols, which refuses to waste the talents of half the population, is thus amply attested in the first three chapters of the *History*. But our final text, Polo-Rustichello's, will offer up the most memorable Mongol woman of all, a woman whose power did not derive from being any-one's wife or mother: the extraordinary Khutulun.

Teaching Marco Polo's/Rustichello of Pisa's *Description of the World*

Le Divisement du Monde, or *The Description of the World*, a late-thirteenth-century composition by a Venetian merchant and an Arthurian romancer, is so richly capacious a text, and so famous, that the name *Marco Polo* is now suborned by restaurants, carpet vendors, ships, and spacecraft, as a touchstone for the exotic, travel, and the East. The text is a fine companion to teach alongside the *Secret History*, since it helps students see what happens to the Mongol Empire, forged in the early thirteenth century by Genghis Khan, once China is incorporated into the Empire by Genghis' grandson, Kublai.

Since I've written extensively on this text, in chapter 6 of *Invention of Race* – especially on race, mercantile capitalism, gender/sexuality, and how a European mercantile gaze itemizes a multifarious world and its people, places, and things into inventories for exchange and profit – I only want to focus here on two themes that integrate the text into my syllabus.[132]

First, we see that like Abu Zayd, Polo-Rustichello has no difficulty whatso-ever accepting the humanity of foreign others when trade and profit are among the benefits of encounter. Indeed, the text's wide-eyed reverence for Yuan China and its Great Khan, Kublai, is boundless: China is the greatest civilization on earth, its emperor the most powerful ruler by any measure (113, 124, *passim*).

---

[132] Elements are highly compact studies; I urge readers to consult the longer-form ideas and arguments in *Race*. Page numbers I cite refer to Latham's translation.

The capital city, Beijing ("Khanbalik"), daily sees a thousand cartloads of silk; the port-city of Hangzhou ("Kinsai") has tax revenues so vast as to be nearly incalculable, though the text gamely calculates these at "14,700,000 gold pieces" (130, 229).

China's cities are magnificent, and students may enjoy comparing them with Vijayanagar and Cairo. Like Vijayanagar, Beijing has professional sex workers, 20,000 of them, and quarters for merchants, grouped by countries of origin (129–130). Hangzhou (which also has beautifully dressed and perfumed ladies-of-the-night) is one of the world's great wonders: surrounded by water, like Venice, but with 12,000 bridges, 3,000 public baths, and 1,600,000 houses; humming with multitudinous entertainments and goods, and evincing such massive prosperity, it seems the greatest city of the thirteenth-century world (215–216, 214–229).

A global-facing, cosmopolitan China, of course, sits on a bedrock of precocious modernity. China has paper money as legal tender: a currency that's a marvel of efficiency, ensuring standardization and ease of conveyance, being neither heavy nor cumbersome like metal money, and guaranteed by a central authority and universally accepted throughout *Pax Mongolica* (147–149).

Paper money ushers in a vision of a world where fiscal exchange, in the form of a lightweight, uniform currency, is standardized, regulated, and universalized: a vision of modernity in a premodern era. The success of paper – a medium with no intrinsic value, but only symbolic and exchange value – depends on a willingness to accept currency as an *abstraction*: a first step toward the even more abstract forms of currency in circulation today, now vanishing into bitcoin, cash apps, and instant transfers.

Like Abu Zayd's Tang China, Polo-Rustichello's Yuan China also has a disaster relief and welfare system. Kublai commutes annual taxes for those with agricultural or husbandry losses, and furnishes the afflicted with replacement stock; he, too, maintains silos of grain, hedged against famine and inflation, releasing grain at cut-rate prices as needed (155, 157–158).

The Yuan state, like the Tang, feeds and sustains the poor, sets up schools for boys, and has an impressive system of registering births that ensures efficient surveillance for taxation and governmental purposes (157–158, *Race* 404 n.131, 227).

The postal system is a marvel, with trunk roads webbing the empire, inter-linking post-stations, horses, and lodgings for those carrying communications, all routinized and systematized into engineered dependability (150–155). Trees are even planted by highways for the comfort and convenience of messengers and merchants (155–156).

While Mongol-ruled China benefits from, perhaps improving on, infrastructure and institutional systems already in place in Tang China centuries before, Mongol modernity is nonetheless memorably differentiated, and uniquely exemplified by an extraordinary woman: the historical personage known as *Khutulun* or *Aiuyurug,* among her historically attested names (spelled *Aiyaruk* in the Penguin translation).

In sharp opposition to all the women depicted in Polo-Rustichello, and, indeed, all the women depicted in our global texts – *Sundiata*, the *Vinland Sagas*, the *Malay Annals*, the *Secret History,* among others – Khutulun is never seen in the role of mother, wife, or sister. Her accomplishments are not the female heroisms traditionally attributed to mothers, wives, and sisters, which praise women for their support of men.

Instead, Khutulun, the daughter of Kaidu, the Khan of the Chagatai Khanate, is a fearless warrior: undefeated in combat, and so strong none could vanquish her (317). She even excels in wrestling – a favorite competitive sport of Mongols, in which death might be the outcome if you lose, as attested in the *Secret History.*

When we meet her, Khutulun is wholly in control of her sexuality and her life. Apparently excelling in psychological relations, she has successfully wrested an agreement from her father, the ruler of Central Asia, that it would be she, not he, who would decide the conditions under which she might consider marrying. Those conditions are deceptively simple: She will not marry anyone who cannot defeat her in hand-to-hand combat. To attempt to defeat her, a contestant must stake 100 horses as his bet.

Since she has amassed 10,000 horses when we meet her, we find that not only does the woman excel at this favorite masculine sport – having already beaten a hundred men – but she has become wealthy from her success. An unvanquished warrior and wrestler, this princess is apparently an economic agent par excellence, in a text that admires economic resourcefulness and wealth.

Polo-Rustichello is clearly fascinated with this woman, who so spectacularly fails to conform to gender expectations, yet is seemingly not punished for her deviance from gender norms. Thus confounded, the text describes one final attempt at getting her married, when a princely suitor – young, comely, strong, powerful, right in every way – brings with him a fine company, and 1,000 fine horses as his stake. Nobody had ever matched him in strength before, we learn (318).

Everyone in the court, it seems, excitedly roots for him, even Khutulun's parents. Attuned as we are to narrative conventions laid down by mytho-literary characters like Atalanta or Brünhilde – virgins who are somehow tricked, and/or must succumb to a man who will take their virginity – we expect story conventions to incline toward a happy ending of female defeat, followed by grand marriage festivities.

But Khutulun handily defeats this paragon of male perfection, throwing him onto the palace floor and winning his 1,000 "very fine" horses. The text rubs it in a little: "such was his grief and shame . . . he lost no time in departing . . . bitterly mortified and ashamed that after finding no man who could stand against him he should be worsted by a woman" (318, 319). Our last glimpse of Khutulun shows her again in many battles, where, we learn, she had a habit of charging into enemy lines, and seizing and bringing back captives by force (319).

Polo-Rustichello omits this, but the historical Khutulun is believed to have eventually married, choosing her own husband freely, having two sons, and eventually turning down her father's wish for her to become Khan after his death, because she preferred to continue leading the military, and supporting her brother Orus as successor instead (*Race* 404–405 n.132). Vilified by some chroniclers, who scurrilously hoot misogynist accusations at her, Polo-Rusticello shows this indomitable woman never being criticized in any way – not by those around her, and not by the text.[133]

Historians today tell us that warrior women were always part of Mongol armies (Weatherford 121). A Dominican friar's and an archbishop's letters between 1234 and 1238 report that a Mongol princess led an army into Russian cities, according to terrified refugees; Thomas of Spalato, describing the invasion of Dalmatia and the siege of Split in 1242, tells us that "many women fought in the Mongol army and were braver and wilder than the men" (Weatherford 121). Adrienne Mayor's *The Amazons*, based on archeological data, also features Khutulun, and other steppe warrior women.

Ending the semester with the vision of Khutulun, last seen in the text still undefeated in battle, and the foremost champion of the army, someone who fearlessly captures enemies, as she disappears into history, is one way to attest to the surprises of premodernity and its global texts (319). While the vision of Khutulun may not answer to every wish we might have, as we encounter the global past, there will be students in your classroom who will find it satisfying enough.

9 The Role/s of Students in the Early Global Literature Classroom: Taking Ownership of the Course, Research, and Team Projects

In my guidelines to teaching early global literatures, I've suggested that students be asked to follow topics, characterizations, and themes which are close to their heart – whether these involve women, sexuality, children, kin relations, race, Orientalism, bridges-across-difference, climate or environmental conditions,

---

[133] Students might wish to compare Khutulun's remarkable depiction here with her epigonic depiction in *Turandot*, the opera based on her story that transforms her strength and prowess into a silly contest of three riddles that lead to marital reward for the opera's unlikable male protagonist.

courts, festivities and celebrations, food, arts and artisanry, animals, plants, global cities, religious beliefs, merchants, militaries, diplomacy, modes of travel, or something else – as they read the texts of the semester.

Doing this, by semester's end, students will have acquired a rich comparative understanding of what their focal interest looks like across the myriad cultures and societies of the world.

For them to compile a comparative understanding of this kind, it helps greatly if students are not also anxiously focused on tests, quizzes, and exams throughout the semester and at semester's end. To those who believe that learning must always involve testing, I respectfully suggest that the global literature classroom might be precisely the space in which to let go of any well-intentioned aims for students to absorb, then regurgitate back, information.

Rather, the global literature classroom is an ideal space for inviting students to contribute to their learning experience by undertaking research, and sharing what they find: and, in this way, take ownership of the course through the generation of course content. Undergraduates are usually excited to conduct research, when the prompt is to follow their curiosity and passions.

Is someone curious about how mercantile relations are sustained over vast distances in an era where no international laws exist to protect business transactions? This is an opportunity to explore the use of *fictive kinships* and what they accomplish, and the importance of a society's prestige, influence, and reach. Fascinated by how universal *alcohol* seems to be, like death and taxes, and how each place finds its own ways to ferment intoxicants? Other inquiring minds in the class will want to know. Surprised at how different premodern slavery is from unfreedom in later eras? Here's the chance to delve deeply into enslavement in a particular region.

Students with a love of music can research the griots of Mali and their instruments, or the throat-singing of the Mongols. A Muslim student might offer a presentation on Quranic recitation, or the jurisprudential schools of Islam, to amplify Ibn Fadlan's perspective.[134] Those keen on cities can explore the shape of architectural and urban design, temples, mosques, or hostelries, while foodies focus on spices, luxury foods, iconic cuisines. The geographically minded can compare maps from different civilizations, the artistically minded can delve into textiles, pigments, precious stones, traveling motifs and patterns.

---

[134] A student, Ella Johnsen, fascinated by how Ibn Fadlan saw time as the duration needed for reading one-seventh of the Quran, decided to research the experience of time, and the invention of clocks, in different cultures. One reviewer of this Element recommends experiential digital projects: "Have students play and critique the Discovery Tour of Assassin's Creed Valhalla," or students could "collaboratively create their own village inspired by the work of Jeffrey Fleisher (mentioned in note 46) in Minecraft Education … often available at low or no cost at universities that use Microsoft products."

Some might research games and sports like Mongol wrestling. One group of undergrads, after reading the *Malay Annals*, excitedly wrote a term paper on Southeast Asian folklore and mythology – a superb paper of near-publishable quality.

In following their interests, of course, students must be free to accomplish multidisciplinary investigation, rather than be confined to literature alone. And, beyond supplying important backgrounds that thicken our understanding of the semester's texts, they must be free to explore cultures and places untouched by the syllabus – say, sea voyaging in Oceania, or plant domesticates in Mesoamerica, or the traditions of the Inuit and the Saami. Doing this produces a deeply layered, richly multifarious sense of the world far beyond our texts, and, since we cannot encompass every place on the planet through texts alone, student contributions of this kind are an especially important part of course content.

It's therefore imperative, at the beginning of a semester, to invite students to take ownership of the global literature course and make it their own: to have them know that *they* have important responsibility for course content too, and important contributions to make. I ask students to share their research and participate in the teaching/learning process through an in-class presentation, and a collaborative term paper. When someone understands they will be actively teaching others, while they themselves are also learning, the classroom culture that forms is energetic and dynamic.

Even those who are shy, or unaccustomed to standing before a class for a solo presentation, agree that learning to do this, in college, is helpful later, when the chances of having to stand before an audience and talk, especially in job-related contexts, are quite high. Disability accommodations, of course, are always possible: A student may elect to make a presentation remotely, rather than in person; have a friend present their work for them; or, if necessary, email a presentation, and answer questions remotely.

Because they belong to a multimedia generation, my students tend to produce PowerPoint presentations, with images, text, sound; maps or tables; and often, audiovisual clips or short YouTube segments. Some may read from a prepared text or cards, while the confident might speak extempore. From many years of student presentations, I can report that, if you help students select a topic they are enthusiastic about and provide clear guidelines as to what the research and presentation should involve, most in-class presentations will be excellent.

At semester's end, a student may research and write a term paper by themselves, of course, and some are eager to do this. But an excellent community-building exercise is to have students form pods, or small groups, to conduct research and writing.[135] Employers are often impressed when a young person has experience in successfully working in a group, is comfortable with negotiating different personalities and temperaments, and able to contribute to a substantial outcome. Often, the members of a pod will have different talents – some being especially good at formulating questions, others at research, writing, or editing – with pod leaders often chosen by the group for superior skills in coordination.

Pod leaders report back on their group's progress throughout the semester, so that you can oversee and guide their progress. At semester's end, each group then shares their accomplished project in a presentation to the whole class, so that everyone can see what everyone else has worked on, and all the researchers receive the plaudits of their peers. Thinking, researching, and writing together like this, some of my students have forged long-term friendships, remaining friends with their group long after class is over.

My evaluations show that students keenly value what they learn from accomplishing research and from listening to the research of their peers: They find these experiences to be among the most rewarding of the semester. For you, the instructor, when students become your active collaborators, no high pedagogical perch whence you must know-it-all, and tell-it-all, is necessary. Traversing the world together in this collective way, in texts and projects, will bring surprises, pleasures, and satisfactions you cannot anticipate.

Who could ask for more, from a teaching experience that never ceases to be a learning experience?

---

[135] Creative writing projects can also offer rich research opportunities. As I write this, one collaborative pod is preparing a collection of composite fictional lives, inspired by Susan Whitfield's *Life along the Silk Road*, with personalities ranging from an innkeeper to a merchant-slaver.

Works Cited

Adler, Marcus Nathan, ed. and trans. *The Itinerary of Benjamin of Tudela: Critical Text, Translation and Commentary*. Oxford University Press, 1907.

trans. *The Itinerary of Benjamin of Tudela*. Introductions by A. Asher (1840), Marcus Nathan Adler (1907), and Michael A. Signer (1983). Joseph Simon/Pangloss Press, 1983.

Almqvist, Bo. "'My Name is Guðriðr': An Enigmatic Episode in *Grœnlendinga saga*." In *Approaches to Vínland*. Ed. Andrew Wawn and Þórunn Sigurdardóttir. Sigurður Nordal Institute, 2001, pp. 15–30.

Atwood, Christopher, trans. *The Secret History of the Mongols*. Penguin, 2023.

Baker, Mona, ed. *Critical Readings in Translation Studies*. Routledge, 2010.

Barker, Hannah. *That Most Precious Merchandise: The Mediterranean Trade in Black Sea Slaves, 1260–1500*. University of Pennsylvania Press, 2019.

Bartlet, Suzanne (with Patricia Skinner). *Licoricia of Winchester: Marriage, Motherhood and Murder in the Medieval Anglo-Jewish Community*. Valentine Mitchell, 2009.

Belcher, Stephen. *Epic Traditions of Africa*. Indiana University Press, 1999.

Berzock, Kathleen Bickford, ed. *Caravans of Gold, Fragments in Time*. Princeton University Press, 2019.

Binyam, Yonatan and Verena Krebs. *"Ethiopia" and the World, 330–1500 CE*. Cambridge Elements in the Global Middle Ages, Cambridge University Press, 2024. DOI: 10.1017/9781009106115.

Blessing, Patricia, Elizabeth Dospěl Williams, and Eiren L. Shea. *Medieval Textiles across Eurasia, c. 300–1400*. Cambridge Elements in the Global Middle Ages, Cambridge University Press, 2023. DOI: 10.1017/9781009393379.

Borbone, Pier Giorgio, ed. and trans. *History of Mar Yahballaha and Rabban Sauma*. Translated into English by Laura E. Parodi. Verlag Tredition, 2021.

Boyle, John Andrew, trans. *Genghis Khan: The History of the World Conqueror by Ata-Malik Juvaini*. Manchester University Press, 1977.

trans. *The Successors of Genghis Khan: Translated from the Persian of Rashid al-Din*. Columbia University Press, 1971.

Broadhurst, Roland J. C., trans. *The Travels of Ibn Jubayr*. Goodwood, 2008; repr. from Jonathan Cape, 1952.

Brown, C. C., trans. *Sejarah Melayu or Malay Annals*. Introduction by R. Roolvink. Oxford University Press, 1970. Oxford in Asia Historical Reprints.

Brown, Nancy Marie. *The Far Traveler: Voyages of a Viking Woman*. Mariner, 2008.

Bruchac, Joseph. *The Ice Hearts*. Cold Mountain Press, 1979.

Budge, E. A. Wallis, trans. *The Monks of Kublai Khan, Emperor of China, or The History of the Life and Travels of Rabban Sawma, Envoy and Plenipotentiary of the Mongol Khans to the Kings of Europe, and Markos, who as Mar Yahbhallaha III Became Patriarch of the Nestorian Church in Asia*. The Religious Tract Society, 1928.

Casanova, Pascale. "Consecration and Accumulation of Literary Capital: Translation as Unequal Exchange." *Critical Readings in Translation Studies*, ed. Mona Baker. Routledge, 2010, pp. 287–303.

Cassidy, Caitlin. "Australian Catholic University Sparks Anger over Scrapping Medieval History and Philosophy Departments." *The Guardian*, 14 September 2023. www.theguardian.com/australia-news/2023/sep/14/australian-catholic-university-condemned-over-totally-indefensible-cuts-to-humanities-programs (accessed October 19, 2023).

Chaganti, Seeta. "Solidarity and the Medieval Invention of Race," *Cambridge Journal of Postcolonial Literary Inquiry* vol. 9 no. 1, 2022, 122–131.

Cobb, Paul M., trans. Usama ibn Munqidh, *The Book of Contemplation: Islam and the Crusades*. Penguin, 2008.

Condé, Djanka Tassey, griot-jeli, and David Conrad, trans. *Sunjata: A New Prose Version*. Hackett, 2016.

Damrosch, David. *How to Read World Literature*. Second edition, Wiley-Blackwell, 2018.

     ed. *Teaching World Literature*. Options for Teaching series. Modern Language Association of America, 2009.

Davidson, Cathy N. "Strangers on a Train: A Chance Encounter Provides a Lesson in Complicity and the Never-Ending Crisis in the Humanities." *Academe*, September–October 2001. www.aaup.org/article/strangers-train#.Xu7_1i2ZPOQ (accessed December 5, 2022).

Dawood, N. J., trans. *Tales from the Thousand and One Nights*. Penguin, 1955.

Dawson, Christopher, ed. *Mission to Asia*. University of Toronto Press, 1980.

De Rachewiltz, Igor, trans. *The Secret History of the Mongols: A Mongolian Epic Chronicle of the Thirteenth Century*. 3 vols., Brill, 2004, 2006.

Donoghue, Daniel, ed. *Beowulf: A Verse Translation*. Trans. Seamus Heaney. Norton Critical Editions series. W. W. Norton, 2019.

Freedman, Marci. "Teaching Benjamin of Tudela's *Book of Travels* and the Jewish Middle Ages." In *Teaching the Global Middle Ages*, ed. Geraldine Heng. Options for Teaching series. Modern Language Association of America, 2022, pp. 85–98.

Freeman-Grenville, G. S. P., ed. and trans. *The Book of the Wonders of India: Mainland, Sea and Islands*. East–West Publications, 1981.

Frye, Richard, trans. *Ibn Fadlan's Journey to Russia: A Tenth-Century Traveler from Baghdad to the Volga River*. Markus Wiener, 2006.

Galbraith, Kate. "British 'Medievalists' Draw Their Swords." *Chronicle of Higher Education*, June 6, 2003, A42.

Ghosh, Amitav. *In an Antique Land: History in the Guise of a Traveler's Tale*. Granta, 1992.

"The Slave of MS. H.6." *Subaltern Studies VII: Writings on South Asian History and Society*. Ed. Partha Chatterjee and Gyanendra Pandey. Oxford University Press, 1993, pp. 159–220.

Ghosh, Amitav and Dipesh Chakrabarty. "A Correspondence on *Provincializing Europe*," *Radical History Review* vol. 83, Spring 2002, 146–172.

Gibb, H. A. R. and C. F. Beckingham, trans. *The Travels of Ibn Battutah*. Abridged, introduced, and annotated by Tim Mackintosh-Smith. Picador, 2002. Abridged from the Hakluyt Society's 5 vols.

Goitein, S. D. and Mordechai Akiva Friedman, eds. and trans. *India Traders of the Middle Ages: Documents from the Cairo Geniza* ("India Book"). Brill, 2008.

Gomez, Michael A. *African Dominion: A New History of Empire in Early and Medieval West Africa*. Princeton University Press, 2018.

"*The Epic of Sunjata* and the Changing Worlds of Trans-Saharan Africa." In *Teaching the Global Middle Ages*, ed. Geraldine Heng. Modern Language Association of America, 2022, pp. 147–162.

Haddawy, Husain, trans. *The Arabian Nights*. W. W. Norton, 1990.

Hamdun, Said and Noël King, trans. *Ibn Battuta in Black Africa*. Markus Wiener, 1998.

Hart, Roger. *The Chinese Roots of Linear Algebra*. Johns Hopkins University Press, 2011.

Hartman, Saidiya. "Venus in Two Acts," *Small Axe* vol. 12, no. 2, 2008, 1–14.

Hartwell, Robert. "A Cycle of Economic Change in Imperial China: Coal and Iron in Northeast China, 750–1350." *Journal of the Social and Economic History of the Orient* vol. 10, 1967, 102–159.

"A Revolution in the Chinese Iron and Coal Industries during the Northern Sung, 960–1126 A.D." *Journal of Asian Studies* vol. 21, no. 2, Feb. 1962, 153–162.

Haverkamp-Rott, Eva. "Jewish History or History of the Jews as Global History." In *Teaching the Global Middle Ages*, ed. Geraldine Heng. Options for Teaching series. Modern Language Association of America, 2022, pp. 218–248.

Heller-Roazen, Daniel, sel. and ed., and Husain Haddawy, trans. *The Arabian Nights: A Norton Critical Edition*. W. W. Norton, 2010.

Heng, Derek. *Southeast Asian Interactions: Geography, Networks, and Trade*. Cambridge Elements in the Global Middle Ages, Cambridge University Press, 2022, DOI:10.1017/9781108907095.

"Teaching the *Malay Annals*, or Southeast Asia in the World." In *Teaching the Global Middle Ages*, ed. Geraldine Heng. Modern Language Association of America, 2022, pp. 207–217.

Heng, Geraldine. "An Experiment in Collaborative Humanities: Imagining the World 500–1500." *ADFL Bulletin* vol. 38 no. 3, 2007, 20–28.

"Global Interconnections: Imagining the World 500–1500," *Medieval Academy Newsletter*, September 2004.

"The Global Middle Ages," *Experimental Literary Education*, Special Issue of *English Language Notes* vol. 47 no. 1, 2009, 205–216.

The Global Middle Ages: An Introduction. Cambridge Elements in the Global Middle Ages, Cambridge University Press, 2021. DOI: 10.1017/ 9781009161176.

ed. *Teaching the Global Middle Ages*. Options for Teaching series. Modern Language Association of America, 2022.

The Invention of Race in the European Middle Ages. Cambridge University Press, 2018.

"An Ordinary Ship and Its Stories of Early Globalism: Modernity, Mass Production, and Art in the Global Middle Ages." *The Journal of Medieval Worlds* vol. 1 no. 1, 2019, 11–54.

Hennessey, William O., trans. *Proclaiming Harmony*. The University of Michigan Center for Chinese Studies, 1981. *Michigan Papers in Chinese Studies* no. 41.

Jackson, Peter, and David Morgan, ed. *The Mission of Friar William of Rubruck: His Journey to the Court of the Great Khan Mongkë 1253–1255*. Trans. Peter Jackson. Haklyut Society, 1990. Repr. Hackett, 2009.

Jansson, Sven B. F., ed. *Sagorna om Vinland: Handscrifterna till Erik den rödes saga*. Vol. 1. Hakan Ohlssons Boktryckeri, 1944.

Johnston, Neil. "Leicester University Considers Lessons in Diversity as Medieval Studies Axed." *The Sunday Times*, February 5, 2021, www .thetimes.co.uk/article/leicester-university-considers-lessons-in-diversity-as-medieval-studies-axed-nsrs2hvf0 (accessed September 26, 2022).

Jones, Gywn, trans. *Eirik the Red, and Other Icelandic Sagas*. Oxford University Press, 1961.

Khalidi, Tarif, trans. "Al-Jahiz, The Boasts of the Blacks Over the Whites." *Islamic Quarterly* vol. 25 no. 1, 1981, 4–51.

Kim, Dorothy. "White Supremacists Have Weaponized an Imaginary Viking Past. It's Time to Reclaim the Real History." *Time*, April 14, 2019, https://time.com/5569399/viking-history-white-nationalists/ (accessed September 26, 2022).

Kingdom of Heaven. Twentieth Century Fox, 2007.

Kinoshita, Sharon, trans. *Marco Polo: The Description of the World*. Hackett, 2016.

Kouyaté, Djeli Mamoudou, griot/jeli, Djibril Tamsir Niane, trans. (French), and G. D. Pickett, trans. (English). *Sundiata: An Epic of Old Mali*. Longman, 1965. Repr. edition. 2006. Longman African Writers.

Kunz, Keneva, trans. "The Vinland Sagas." In *The Sagas of Icelanders: A Selection*. Penguin, 2001, pp. 626–674.

Kusimba, Chapurukha M. *Swahili Worlds in Globalism*. Cambridge Elements in the Global Middle Ages, Cambridge University Press, 2023. DOI: 10.1017/9781009072922.

Lambourn, Elizabeth A. *Abraham's Luggage: A Social Life of Things in the Medieval Indian Ocean World*. Cambridge University Press, 2018.

Latham, Ronald, trans. *The Travels of Marco Polo*. Penguin, 1958. Reissued and reprinted several times.

Legge, James, trans. *A Record of Buddhistic Kingdoms: Being an Account by the Chinese Monk Fâ-Hien of His Travels in India and Ceylon (A.D. 399–414) in Search of the Buddhist Books of Discipline*. 1886; repr. Paragon/Dover, 1965.

Li, Rongxi, trans. *The Great Tang Dynasty Record of the Western Regions* (Xuanzang (*ca.* 602–664). Numata Center for Buddhist Translation and Research, 1996.

Lomuto, Sierra. "Public Medievalism and the Rigor of Anti-Racist Critique." *In the Middle*, April 4, 2019, www.inthemedievalmiddle.com/2019/04/public-medievalism-and-rigor-of-anti.html (accessed September 26, 2022).

Mackintosh-Smith, Tim, ed. and trans. *Accounts of China and India*. In *Two Arabic Travel Books*, New York University Press, 2014, pp. 4–161.

Magnusson, Magnus and Herman Pálsson, trans. *The Vinland Sagas: The Norse Discovery of America*. Penguin, 1965.

Mayor, Adrienne. *The Amazons: Lives and Legends of Warrior Women across the Ancient World*. Princeton University Press, 2014.

Mongol: The Rise of Genghis Khan. New Line, 2008.

Montgomery, James A., trans. *The History of Yaballaha III, Nestorian Patriarch, and of His Vicar Bar Sauma, Mongol Ambassador to the*

Frankish Courts at the End of the Thirteenth Century. Columbia University Press, 1927.

Montgomery, James E., ed. and trans. Ahmad ibn Fadlan, *Mission to the Volga*. New York University Press, 2017.

ed. and trans. Ahmad ibn Fadlan, *Mission to the Volga*. In *Two Arabic Travel Books*, New York University Press, 2014, pp. 165–297.

Moule, A. C. *Christians in China before the Year 1550*. Society for Promoting Christian Knowledge, 1930, pp. 94–127.

Moule, A. C. and Paul Pelliot, ed. and trans. *Marco Polo: The Description of the World*. 2 vols. Routledge, 1938.

Ng, Su Fang. *Alexander the Great from Britain to Southeast Asia: Peripheral Empires in the Global Renaissance*. Oxford University Press, 2019.

Ong, Natalie S. Y. "Style and Substance: Investigating the Gold Ornaments of Ancient Temasek." *International Institute for Asian Studies Newsletter* 94, Spring 2023: www.iias.asia/the-newsletter/article/style-and-substance-investigating-gold-ornaments-ancient-temasek (accessed February 20, 2025).

Prange, Sebastian R. *Monsoon Islam: Trade and Faith on the Medieval Malabar* Coast. Cambridge University Press, 2018.

Preston, William, ed., Vincent J. Cornell, trans. Al-Jahiz. *The Book of the Glory of the Black Race*. Preston Collection, 1991.

Qitsualik-Tinsley, Rachel and Sean. *Skraelings*. Inhabit Media, 2014.

Rambaran-Olm, Mary. "Anglo-Saxon Studies [Early English Studies], Academia, and White Supremacy." *Medium*, June 27, 2018, https://mrambaranolm.medium.com/anglo-saxon-studies-academia-and-white-supremacy-17c87b360bf3 (accessed September 26, 2022).

Rambaran-Olm, Mary and Erik Wade. "What's in a Name? The Past and Present Racism in 'Anglo-Saxon' Studies." *The Yearbook of English Studies*, vol. 22, 2022, 135–153.

Ronchi, Gabriella, ed. *Milione: Le devisement dou monde*. Il milione nelle redazioni Toscana e franco-italiana. Mondadori, 1982.

Seale, Yasmine, trans. *The Annotated Arabian Nights*. Ed. Paulo Lemos Horta. Norton 2021.

Sisòkò, Fa-Digi, griot-jeli, and John William Johnson, trans. *The Epic of Son-Jara: A West African Tradition*. Indiana University Press, 1992.

Son-Jara: The Mande Epic. Mandekan/English Edition with Notes and Commentary. Indiana University Press, 1986. Third edition, 2003.

Standaert, Nicolas. *Handbook of Christianity in China, Vol. I: 635–1800*. Brill, 2001.

Sveinsson, Einar, and Matthías Þórðarson, ed. "Grœnlendinga saga." *Íslenzk Fornrit* vol. 4. Íslenzka Fornritafélag, 1935, pp. 239–269.

The Story of the Weeping Camel. Tobias Siebert, 2004.

Thackston, W. M., trans. Kamaluddin Abdul-Razzaq Samarqandi. *Mission to Calicut and Vijayanagar.* In *A Century of Princes: Sources on Timurid History and Art.* Aga Khan Program for Islamic Architecture, 1989, pp. 299–232.

The Thirteenth Warrior. Touchstone Pictures, 1999.

Weatherford, Jack. *The Secret History of the Mongol Queens.* Broadway, 2010.

Whitaker, Cord. "*The Invention of Race* and the Status of Blackness." *Cambridge Journal of Postcolonial Literary Inquiry* vol. 9 no. 1, 2022, 149–158.

Whitfield, Roderick, ed. and Matthew Wegehaupt, trans., *Korean Buddhist Culture: Accounts of a Pilgrimage, Monuments, and Eminent Monks.* In *Collected Works of Korean Buddhism.* Vol. 10, ed. Roderick Whitfield. Jogye Order of Korean Buddhism, 2015, pp. 5–174.

Whitfield, Susan. *Life Along the Silk Road.* University of California Press, 2001. Second edition, 2015.

Wilson, Jason. "Suspect in Portland Double Murder Posted White Supremacist Material Online." *The Guardian*, 28 May, 2017. https://www.theguardian .com/us-news/2017/may/27/portland-double-murder-white-supremacist-muslim-hate-speech (accessed February 20, 2025).

Wyngaert, Anastasius van den, ed. *Sinica Franciscana, Vol. I: Itinera et Relationes Fratrum Minorum saec. XIII et XIV.* Franciscan Press, 1929.

Yang, Han-Sung, Yun-Hua Jan, Lida Shotaro, and Laurence Preston, ed. and trans. *The Hye Ch'o Diary: Memoir of the Pilgrimage to the Five Regions of India.* Asian Humanities Press and Po Chin Chai, 1984.

Young, Helen and Kavita Mudan Finn. *Global Medievalism: An Introduction.* Cambridge Elements in the Global Middle Ages, Cambridge University Press, 2022. DOI: 10.1017/9781009119658.

Teaching Early Global Literatures and Cultures is dedicated to the late **Suporn Arriwong**, most beloved and dearest of students, who left too soon, to the devastation of all:

Epitaph

by Merrit Malloy

When I die, give what's left of me away
To children and old people who wait to die.

If you need to cry,
Cry for your brother and sister
Walking the street beside you.
And when you need me,
Put your arms around anyone and
Give them what you need to give to me.

I want to leave you something,
Something better than words or sounds.
Look for me in the people I've known or loved.
If you cannot give me away,
At least let me live in your eyes,
And not in your mind.

You can love me most
By letting hands touch hands,
By letting hearts touch hearts.
And by letting go of
Spirits who need to be free.

Love does not die, bodies do.
So, when all that's left of me is love,
Give me away.

Cambridge Elements

The Global Middle Ages

Geraldine Heng

University of Texas at Austin

Geraldine Heng is Mildred Hajek Vacek and John Roman Vacek Chair of English and Comparative Literature at the University of Texas, Austin. She is the author of *The Invention of Race in the European Middle Ages* (2018), *England and the Jews: How Religion and Violence Created the First Racial State in the West* (2019), and *The Global Middle Ages: An Introduction* (2021), all published by Cambridge University Press, as well as *Empire of Magic: Medieval Romance and the Politics of Cultural Fantasy* (2003, Columbia). She is the editor of *Teaching the Global Middle Ages* (2022, MLA), coedits the University of Pennsylvania Press series, RaceB4Race: Critical Studies of the Premodern, and is working on a new book, Early Globalisms: The Interconnected World, 500–1500 CE. Originally from Singapore, Heng is a Fellow of the American Academy of Arts and Sciences, a Fellow of the Medieval Academy of America, a member of the Medievalists of Color, and Founder and Codirector, with Susan Noakes, of the Global Middle Ages Project: www.globalmiddleages.org.

Susan J. Noakes

University of Minnesota–Twin Cities

Susan J. Noakes is Professor of French and Italian at the University of Minnesota–Twin Cities, where she also serves as Chair of the Department of French and Italian. For her many publications in French, Italian, and comparative literature, the university in 2009 named her Inaugural Chair in Arts, Design, and Humanities. Her most recent publication is an analysis of Salim Bachi's *L'Exil d'Ovide*, exploring a contemporary writer's reflection on his exile to Europe by comparing it to Ovid's exile to the Black Sea; it appears in *Salim Bachi*, edited by Agnes Schaffhauser, published in Paris by Harmattan in 2020.

Lynn Ramey

Vanderbilt University

Lynn Ramey is Professor of French and Cinema and Media Arts at Vanderbilt University and Chair of the Department of French and Italian. She is the author of *Jean Bodel: An Introduction* (2024, University Press of Florida), *Black Legacies: Race and the European Middle Ages* (2014, University Press of Florida), and *Christian, Saracen and Genre in Medieval French Literature* (2001, Routledge). She is currently working on recreations of medieval language, literature, and culture in video games for which she was awarded an NEH digital humanities advancement grant in 2022.

About the Series

Elements in the Global Middle Ages is a series of concise studies that introduce researchers and instructors to an uncentered, interconnected world, c. 500–1500 CE. Individual Elements focus on the globe's geographic zones, its natural and built environments, its cultures, societies, arts, technologies, peoples, ecosystems, and lifeworlds.

Cambridge Elements ≡

The Global Middle Ages

Elements in the Series

A full series listing is available at: www.cambridge.org/EGMA

Printed in the United States
by Baker & Taylor Publisher Services